WITCHCRAFT Spell Book

The Complete Guide of Witchcraft Rituals and Spells for Beginners

G. Alan Joel

ISBN: 098891123X
ISBN-13: 978-0-9889112-3-9

Bequeathed To

Magical Blessing

Dedication

Disclaimer & Legal notice

Contents

Contents – cont'd

CONTENTS – CONT'D

Contents – Cont'd

This Magical Tome
is
Bequeathed To:

____

Magical Blessing

Child of Wonder, Child of Flame
Nourish Our Spirits and Protect Our Aim.
This entire year be filled with the effects
of magically-sown seeds,
Thus our lives be expanded by attitudes of
experimentation and magical deeds!
Upon the foundation of magical and shamanic
practice may we build,
Which keep us safe while carrying us through to what
we have willed!
The year past has been one of building force and
making positive life changes,
While this year present challenges us to renew our
resolve, choosing in all of life's strangeness!
With the aid of the Winds, our Spirits and Old Ones,
We Work with our Totems and intentions until done.
Honoring Magic's proper place,
In the Sixth World embraced by Wisdom and Grace.
Exploring the mystery and places of old,
Searching for the knowledge we seek to unfold.
To defining our aims and honing our skills we aspire
As we quickly succeed in manifesting what we desire.

Dedication

To the pioneering magical and witchcraft practitioners George Dew and Linda Hilshafer of the Church of Seven Arrows. We thank them from the bottom of our hearts for their huge contribution to this way of life. Their research and work have been crucial to the development of the material in this book.

To all those Old Ones who, by one means or other, passed on to us some understanding of what humans have been and can be.

To all of the students over the years who have shown us as much as we may have shown them.

To all those who are even now striving to recover the full range of human awareness and competency in accord with the ecology and energies of the planet, and the requirements of our environment.

To you, the reader of this book, who even now adds to the grace, beauty, and miracle of magic and witchcraft on planet Earth.

Disclaimer & Legal Notice

The Esoteric School of Shamanism and Magic has made every effort, at the time of this writing, that the information contained in this book is as accurate a possible. The publisher and author make no warranties or representation with respect to the completeness, fitness, accuracy, applicability, or appropriateness of this book's contents. This book's information is provided strictly for entertainment and educational purposes. Should you choose to use or apply the ideas provided in this book, you take full responsibility for your own actions. The publisher and author provide no guarantee that your life will improve in any way should you choose to use the information presented in this book. The ability of the information provided in this book to provide self-help and life improvement to the reader is entirely dependent upon the reader. The reader's ability to gain positive results from the information presented in this book is entirely dependent on the amount of time the reader devotes to the application of the material in this book, the willingness of the reader to dedicate time and effort to learning the materials presented in this book, as well as the reader's own belief system, which may help or hinder the reader's ability to benefit from this book's materials. Since each reader differs according to willingness and openness to the information available in this book, the author and publisher cannot guarantee success or improvement for every individual reader. Neither the publisher nor the author assumes responsibility for the reader's actions, or whether the information is used for negative or positive purposes. The information contained in this book is drawn from tribal traditions—both modern and ancient—as well as the author's 30 plus years' experience researching and teaching this material to students. The information in this book is presented as interpreted by the author, and, as such, may or may not be entirely accurate. In no way should the information presented in this book be a substitute as advice from health or mental health professionals. The author is not liable—or in any way responsible—for actions that the reader may or may not take as a result of reading the information contained in this book. The reader assumes full responsibility for his or her own actions and choices with regard to how he or she chooses to use the information in this book. The reader is strongly encouraged to choose to use the information provided in this book responsibly.

1

Some Witchy Thoughts to Think About...

As you read through the various rituals and spells described in this book, you might ask yourself (or you may have already asked yourself) this question:

> *"What do spells and rituals of witchcraft and magic really do for me?"*

Hopefully, by the time you reach the end of this book, you will be able to answer that question for yourself. In the meantime, the following is a short list of benefits you can gain from doing regular witchcraft spells and rituals. Return to this section and re-read it if or when you begin to doubt yourself as you practice the techniques outlined in later sections.

Disrupt the Trance of Everyday Life

Your practice should shift you out of the well-worn mental pathways of your daily life. The spells and rituals you do should make you pause in your day, be conscious and aware of who you are, where you are, and what your aims are. Any spells, consciously performed, should prevent you from being a purely mechanical robot.

Connect You with Spirit

Staying connected to Spirit is essential to attracting what you really want in your life. You can connect with Spirit through any or all of the spells and rituals described in this book. Any spell that quiets the mind or puts us in touch with physical sensation will bring us into contact with Spirit.

Help You Access Powers and Beings

Creating what we want in life is much easier when we have help. A daily practice of witchcraft or magic that puts you in contact with angels, guides, totem Spirits, and other helpers can increase your ability to attract what you want in life. Remember that there is a helpful being for just about anything you want—don't be afraid to ask!

Help You Remember What You Want

Many of us go through our days in a reactionary mode—we are not choosing our thoughts and actions so much as we are reacting to the stimulus around us. Daily performance of magical rituals and spells helps us remember what we really want in life, and keeps us from sabotaging ourselves with unwanted reactions. For instance, if your goal is to create peace and harmony in life, a daily witchcraft practice can keep you in touch with

Spirit, reminding you not to react angrily to your co-worker's insults.

BE IN ACCORDANCE WITH UNIVERSAL PRINCIPLES

Doing daily spells and rituals that are designed with Universal principles in mind is much more effective than those that are not—plus, they are guaranteed to be safe. Sound spells follow Rules of the Road, principles such as "as above, so below," and four element principles. For instance, if you're designing a ritual to help you gain knowledge, you want to work with the principles of the magical element Air. If you want a ritual that will help you act, you want to work with Fire.

SOME OTHER IDEAS TO CONTEMPLATE: TOP 5 REASONS WE DON'T GET WHAT WE WANT IN LIFE

#5: WE THINK WE HAVE TO "MAKE IT HAPPEN"

Having to "make things happen" is difficult—it involves long hours, hard work, and lots of worry. Thinking about making things happen makes most of us tired, so we just stop trying.

As children, we learned early and often that we have to physically create whatever we want, starting with getting good grades in school so we can get into a good college, get a good job, and live happily ever after. We've got phrases like, "You've got to pull yourself up by your bootstraps" and "If you want something done right, you've got to do it yourself."

The truth is that we do make some things happen, but most of the time we create with the Universe's help. It's like we're sitting in the Universal restaurant and ordering off a menu: "I'd like the new job for an appetizer, the red car well done as an entrée, and a fabulous soul mate for dessert." The Universe takes our order and serves it up—and the only thing we have to pay at the end of the meal is our appreciation and gratitude. Now that's a cheap date!

Did you know that there is an angel, guide, totem, and helper for just about everything in life? Whether you want a new job, a new mate, or just a shift in your life ("three degrees to the right, please"), there is a Universal being just waiting to help you. All you have to do is ask.

Daily rituals remind us that we're just doing the asking, and the Universe (and all its helpful beings) is handling the delivery. These rituals remind us to relax and just ask!

#4: We Are Afraid of Failure

Because we are not taught in school how to attract what we want, and because we don't get a lot of practice, most of us feel that we are failures when it comes to getting what we want. We hate failure, so we give up on our desires and just accept whatever meager servings life puts on our plate.

The truth is that we are all fabulous co-creators in collaboration with the Universe, and we never fail. Sometimes we don't create what we want, but we're always creating—we can't help it. Humans are born to create, all the time. What's more, most of the time we do create what we want in life. We just become impatient and move on to our next desires before our first creation has manifested. As a result, we end up settling for less, and never see the results of our original creations!

Rituals of magic and witchcraft bring that creative process up to the conscious level, making us aware of the actual creation sequence. We begin to see the connection between what we ask for and what we get as a result. Once we are aware of this creation process, we become much more confident creators and we pick up those old dreams and desires we abandoned long ago.

#3: We Are Hypnotized by Daily Life

As a society we have become so hypnotized by the hum of daily life that we forget to create consciously. If you want to see how hypnotic daily life is, check in with your thoughts first thing in the morning and last thing at night. Chances are, your thoughts will be about all the things you have to do during the coming day, or all the things that happened during the past day. Your big desires and dreams probably don't even figure in those thoughts!

Between day planners, smart phones, and tablets, we are sunk up to our eyebrows in the concerns of daily life. We become so engaged in making our daily lives "work" that we forget everything else. We are transformed from humans to robots.

A magical or witchcraft practice can help us create contact with Spirit, and maintain that contact throughout the day. Our Spirits are the keepers of our dreams, desires, and life lessons. When we are in touch with Spirit, we remember ourselves and why we are in body on this planet. Spirit keeps us in touch with our Spirit path, and helps us walk through our daily lives with purpose and meaning. When we are Spirit-led, we are no longer hypnotized by daily life, but use the tools of daily life to achieve our Spirit dreams.

#2: Negativity is Popular

If you've been around the metaphysical community at all, you've probably heard about the principle that we attract into our lives what we focus on. In other words, the sum of our thoughts and feelings (both positive and negative) create the events and people in our lives. So if you want to create your desires in life, all you have to do is think positive thoughts and feel positive vibes. Sounds simple, right?

Unfortunately, in our society it's easier said than done. Negativity is so popular in our society that we're often branded as "Pollyannas" if we're too upbeat and popular. Just turn on the TV and watch any news program or sitcom. The news programs report mainly on disasters or gloom and doom predictions, while the sitcoms are all about characters insulting each other with sarcastic remarks.

We've become so accustomed to these negative forms of communication that it actually feels odd to think, feel, and act in a positive way. Being positive means we have a hard time fitting into the gossipy conversations that have become the norm in daily life.

The good news is that witchcraft rituals, done regularly, move us out of the negative spheres of influence and attract similarly positive people and events into our lives. These rituals give us the extra courage and confidence to stand in the positive flow of consciousness rather than the negative. Plus, they help us remember our dreams, and to think and feel in alignment with those dreams.

#1: We Don't Believe We Can Be, Do, and Have Everything We Want

With phrases like, "You can't have your cake and eat it, too," who can blame us for giving up on our dreams? We're taught that whenever we want something, we have to give up something else.

The truth is that this Universe is limitless from the human perspective. We can ask for and create anything and everything we want, and there is still enough left over for everyone else. We live in a continuously expanding Universe, where we are all creating more and more and more. As humans, we can't ask for enough creation to exceed the Universal limit.

Our job as humans is to create. We are here to experience the process of creation, of being, doing, and having everything we want. Rituals of witchcraft or magic connect us with Universal helpers who can assist us in the process. These rituals also connect us with the understanding that the Universe is limitless, and we can keep asking to our heart's content!

2

IS WITCHCRAFT REAL?

"Is witchcraft real?"

"Is magic real?"

We get these questions multiple times per day. In fact, in recent times requests for this kind of information are increasing exponentially. People desperately want to believe that witchcraft, magic, spell work, and rituals are real. They also want to know whether these esoteric practices are effective for solving life questions. These are all great questions, and we have a single answer for you:

YES.

Witchcraft is real. Magic is real. Spell work does work. Daily magical rituals can improve your life and resolve daily life problems. What you pay into your magical or witchcraft practice pays you back. In other words:

"It's all good!"

But don't take our word for it. In fact, we never want you to take anything this in this book as gospel or truth. The entire basis of the way that we teach witchcraft and magic is ***hypothesis***. In other words, we suggest that you first read about the spells and rituals in this book. Next, that you try the spells and rituals in this book *exactly* as they are described, since witchcraft and magic are precision sciences. In fact:

> ***Altered procedures produce altered results! (more on this later!)***

Finally, you decide *for yourself* whether witchcraft is real. You figure out, based on your own ***experience and observation*** whether spell work really does work. You learn, through daily experience, whether daily magical rituals are useful and helpful in *your* life. You decide. It's all up to you.

> ***We know that witchcraft and magic are real. Your job, in doing the spells and rituals in this book, is to figure out for yourself whether these practices are real... and whether they really work for you.***

In our three decades of teaching, we have discovered that many people can "believe" us when we tell them that magic and witchcraft are real, yet remain unconvinced at a deep level.

The only way for you to believe in witchcraft and magic is for you to try it, do it, play with it, make room for it, open the door for it... and then watch the miracles manifest before your eyes. At that point, we don't need to offer you any words. You will have your own proof and experience with which you will *know* that these practices are real, effective, and useful in daily practical life.

ON HARRY POTTER AND OTHER FICTIONAL MAGICAL SOURCES

While there are certain principles, practices, witchcraft rituals, and magical tools that have some passing resemblance to what you might read in a *Harry Potter* book or see in the movie, *Crouching Tiger, Hidden Dragon*, what we offer you here are practical, proven, and effective spells and rituals that follow Universal Laws.

The same cannot be said of everything in the *Harry Potter* books. For instance, the magical Wand is useful for channeling the element Air, which is associated with messages, communication, thinking, or planning. On the other hand, the Wand is terrible for conducting Fire energies. Why? Because in reality the majority of magical Wands are made of wood, and wood burns.

So while *Harry Potter* is using his Wand as a multi-purpose magical tool to conduct all four magic elements of Air, Fire, Water, and Earth, in truth the Wand can only really channel

Air energies. If you try to throw a lightning bolt (Fire energy) with your Wand, you will find yourself holding a pile of ash, not a Wand. While there are certain Wands, such as those made of iron-wood, which *might* be able to direct a limited amount of Fire energy, ***no Wand*** can continuously conduct all four magical elements on a consistent basis...and survive.

Witchcraft and Magic and You

Witchcraft and magic are very real. These practices have existed as precise sciences for thousands of years. More importantly, every single person can learn to do witchcraft and magic.

We were *all* born with the talents and abilities that empower us to do the rituals and spells in this book. Every single person can do witchcraft and magic.

The only reason that magic and witchcraft seem so, well, miraculous, is that this society no longer teaches these forms of art and science. In the distant past, studies in witchcraft and magic were just as important as math, science, or the arts. In fact, these practices were and still are the birthright of *every* planetary citizen.

That means YOU!

WHAT CAN YOU DO WITH WITCHCRAFT AND MAGIC?

Magic and witchcraft practiced in the real world can be amazing in the changes they can make in people's lives. Magic and witchcraft are first of all precision sciences. These practices are the science of:

- deliberate creation
- effective prayer
- manifesting Higher Will on energetic and material planes
- heightened awareness, selective perception and dynamic, harmonious relationships
- the study of intention (as per Aleister Crowley, one of the greatest magical practitioners of all time)

Every intentional act is a magical act!

Magic and witchcraft are also the study of intention and a system of creation, not coercion.

> ***Note: the word "manipulation" is often used in conjunction with magic, but manipulation simply means the use of the hands. It should be an "OK" word without a lot of charge, but currently it is used mostly to mean coercion. Look it up in a good dictionary!***

Witchcraft and magic allow us to understand the actual workings of the Universe through direct experience, and give us the ability to communicate with beings on all levels.

These practices are also paths of spiritual growth. A practitioner must experience and verify everything for him or herself. Nothing can be taken on blind faith, since there is no blind faith in science!

So what can you actually do with witchcraft and magic?

Quite a lot. Here's a short list to get you started:

- balance your energies for healing and manifestation
- change old beliefs
- defend yourself against physical and psychic attack
- heal yourself and others
- find hidden information and see possible futures
- psychically communicate with other beings
- create sacred space
- find lost people and objects
- manifest what you want and need in life
- much more…

THE FOUR ELEMENTS OF WITCHCRAFT AND MAGIC

At the very basis of these practices is the understanding of the four elements: Air, Fire, Water, and Earth. Called elemental magic, these foundational elements are real. They are the four components that make up the Universe. Air, Fire, Water, and Earth are part of our natural everyday environment. What makes them magical is the understanding of how they operate, not just on the physical level, but also at the levels of mind and Spirit.

For instance, while on the physical level Air is just the stuff we breathe, in the practice of witchcraft and magic Air is the conduit of psychic communication, enlightenment, understanding, dreaming and more. If you want more of any of these things in your life, then you need more magical Air.

How do you get more magical Air? Wear more Air colors, including White for communication and Sky Blue for enlightenment and understanding. To take this one step further, you could also take on more Air by talking to the Owl totem, who lives in the East (the direction of the magical element Air). We will discuss how to work with the Owl totem in a later section of this book.

By just extending your understanding and use of the basic ingredients of nature, you become a practitioner of magic and witchcraft. Seen in this light, these practices are no longer about smoke and mirrors, nor the result of Hollywood special effects. These practices are the result of truly understanding and working with the very elements that are all around you.

YOU'LL SEE IT WHEN YOU BELIEVE IT

Many masters, including Wayne Dyer, have said,

"You'll see it when you believe it."

The same is true for witchcraft and magic. In other words, the suspension of disbelief and the willingness not to exercise contempt prior to investigation are requirements for these practices to be "real" in your life. Magic is all around us—always—but our ability to perceive and use the forces of magic depends on our willingness to be open. No one else can show it to you, only your direct experience and observation can "prove" or demonstrate to you that magic is real.

We've found that one of the simplest ways to experience magic (and your own magical abilities) is to work with beginner spells and rituals, as you are doing by reading this book and doing the procedures described here.

A WORD ON FAITH AND BELIEF VERSUS ACTUAL EXPERIENCE

The word "faith" has always generated a lot of controversy, especially when used in conjunction with religion, magic, witchcraft, God... anything that stirs up the emotions and can rock the very foundation of our souls.

But what is faith really? Is it a belief? Is it a knowingness? Do you have to have faith or belief that magic is real to practice it?

Look up faith in a dictionary and you'll find something like this:

1. confidence or trust in a person or thing: faith in another's ability
2. belief that is not based on proof (he had faith that the hypothesis would be substantiated by fact)

Biblically, faith is "the general persuasion of the mind that a certain statement is true" (dictionary.com). So basically faith is a belief that something is true whether or not there is proof. This is according to standard dictionary definitions... and probably the opinion of the man on the street, too.

But in actuality, faith is action.

THE ABOVE DEFINITION DOESN'T REALLY WORK FOR PRACTITIONERS OF WITCHCRAFT OR MAGIC. TO BELIEVE SOMETHING TO BE TRUE, A PRACTITIONER HAS TO HAVE PERSONALLY OBSERVED OR EXPERIENCED THE PHENOMENON. UNTIL THEN, EVERYTHING REMAINS IN THE CATEGORY OF HYPOTHESIS. THAT'S ALL WELL AND GOOD, BUT THEN HOW DOES SOMEONE—LIKE YOU OR THE

AVERAGE JOE ON THE STREET—FIGURE OUT WHETHER SOMETHING IS TRUE OR WORTHY OF "FAITH"?

You take action!

What we mean is that you develop a daily practice of rituals and/or spells. The beginner spells and rituals in this book are great places to start building your practice. Pick a procedure, any procedure, in this book (or all of them) and do them.

Take action! See for yourself what these magical spells do for you and what effect they have on your life. If you keep an open mind, ask for signs and guidance along the way, and simply remain open to the idea that witchcraft and magic are real, then you will see results... no holds barred!

In the immortal words of Nike, "Just do it!"

Don't bother asking a practitioner whether you should believe in love spells. Don't bother asking a practitioner whether the Tarot is accurate. Why? Because you will only be getting *their* experiences and observations. *Their* stuff may not work for *you.*

You have to determine what is true and not true for you, as a person, as a practitioner... whatever *you* want to be. Whatever you want to have faith in... figure out whether it is true for you first. Here's a little hint and motivation to get you started:

Whatever you pay into your magical practice pays you back... with interest!

What do we really mean by having a magical practice? One way to do a magical practice is to pick a single magical spell or ritual from this book and practice it for 40 days—religiously!

One of the simple rituals you will learn is to hire a parking angel to help you get that perfect parking spot in a busy lot... you know, the parking slot that is right next to the door. There are hundreds of thousands of parking angels out there just *waiting* for a driver such as you to ask for help.

Should you have faith in the concept of a parking angel? Should you believe that a parking angel really wants to help you find a parking place? After all, that sounds like a pretty small act of witchcraft, right? Well, you decide. In fact, you are the only one who *can* decide. Hire a parking angel for 40 days and see what happens, if anything, in your life.

At the end of 40 days of hiring one parking angel per day, ask yourself, "Are parking angels worthy of my faith that witchcraft and magic are real?" Answer the question for yourself. If you find it not worthy of your faith, you have not lost anything except missing out on a few choice parking spaces. That isn't a lot to give up.

At the same time, you *will* have paid into your magical practice... and your practice will eventually pay you back, regardless of whether you decide to have faith in parking angels. The Universe is ultimately fair and a great keeper of accounts.

Any acts of intentions, which are magical acts, are recorded in the Akashic records, and will pay you back, perhaps when you least expect it. If your parking angels are worthy of your faith, you have not only paid into your practice but you have also gained a new magical tool to put in your toolkit! This kind of witchy experiment isn't just good, it's good for you. Best of all, the results—all of them—are yours forever.

WHAT IF WITCHCRAFT OR MAGIC HAS NOT WORKED FOR YOU BEFORE?

Many people write us asking why the spells and rituals we describe do not seem to work for them. Our answer? When the spells and rituals do not work, look in the mirror!

Suppose you have set a magical goal, decided on a spell to use, and performed the necessary steps. You then wait a while, nothing seems to be happening, and then you decide that the spell has failed.

> ***Does this sound familiar? Do you know anyone with this complaint?***

Spells and rituals, when followed according to Rules of the Road (to be described later in this book), and exactly according to the given instructions, always work. The Universe cannot and does not violate its own laws.

But why does a spell or ritual sometimes appear not to work? One of the Universal Laws is free will. Thus, we can countermand our own magical work with our intention. This may include:

- hidden belief that the magic won't work
- too much attachment to the outcome (pushing on a spell, which actually slows it down)

- a hidden part of self that does not want the magic to work (especially in the case of relationship disconnects)
- throwing everything but the kitchen sink at the problem (resulting in spells or rituals interfering with each other)
- asking for too many things at once
- not waiting for enough time to pass to allow results to appear

If you have decided that your spell or ritual has not worked, then take a hard, honest look at yourself and see if anything on the list above could apply to you. You will probably find that one or more of the items above *does* apply to you.

If you truly have no clue why a spell or ritual did not work, you may need to do some divination to discover what happened. If you find you have put too many demands into the spell or done something incorrectly you can take a spell down and redo the procedures. If you performed a spell that does not seem to be working, you may need to look at your procedures and make an adjustment. You may need to re-think the goal or thoroughly re-think through the procedure. All spells and rituals need to be thoroughly planned because altered procedures produce altered results. The more complex the spell, the truer this principle.

What's the solution? Do the magic right and thoroughly, and then let it go. Pick specific points at which you will check progress and make additional adjustments then, otherwise ignore it!

Are Witchcraft and Magic Black, White, or Something Else Altogether?

If you go to Google or Yahoo and type in the word "magick," you'll get a lot of listings for black magick, white magick, chaos magick, sex magick and thousands of other kinds of magick. The same is true of words like "witchcraft," "wicca," "magic," and "paganism."

> ***So are witchcraft and magic black, white, or something else altogether?***

In the experience of most practitioners with some level of training, magic and witchcraft are not black or white, good or evil. Instead, magic and witchcraft are based on an unchanging set of operating principles that are in effect whether you know them or not. Magical laws are like physical laws: they are impersonal, fixed, and completely immune to bargaining.

One of our favorite authors, Paxton Robey, explains it so well in his book *No Time for Karma*. He says,

> ***"The Universe and its rules must be seen as impersonal principle if we are to become self empowered beings.***

Remember the law of gravity. When you jump out of the window, you will go down. On the way down, you might remember about gravity, but the earth will not care one way or the other. Gravity is impersonal so it will not say, 'She is a pretty good person so maybe we should let her down easy.'"

While the idea of impersonal Universal forces can seem cold and unfeeling, the good thing is that these laws are very reliable. Just like the law of gravity, you will never have to doubt or question these laws… ever!

WHAT MAKES WITCHCRAFT OR MAGIC BLACK OR WHITE?

What makes the practice of magic or witchcraft either "black" or "white" is our intent. Remember that these practices are all about the study of intention. Our intention and attention are what direct the forces of magic and witchcraft in one direction or another.

So what do you do when you stumble on a website offering black, white, chaos, or sex magic? Or how about a website offering revenge witchcraft? Use your own experience and observation to decide if what is being offered is really right for you. All types of magic are valid. What is right for you depends on your goals as a practitioner.

In reality, all forms of magic are just specializations in the same field. Magic and witchcraft are such vast areas of study that every particular branch is just a focused shot in the dark. Every branch is simply the results of one or more practitioners trying to find out more about this area or that.

For example, voodoo magic is about using the law, "as above, so below" to create effects in the world. What you do to a voodoo doll (as above), you likewise do to the person the doll represents (so below).

Chaos witchcraft is about using extreme methods to create heightened states of awareness and consciousness. Love spells are about attracting the right person to you, although you have to be very careful *never* to bind anyone with a love spell. The karma you garner when you bind someone with a love spell is so bad that you will wish you had never cast the spell!

SIDE-BANDS OR SIDE-EFFECTS TO AVOID

Above we said that all forms of magic and witchcraft are valid. They are. But some have "side-bands" or side effects that you might want to avoid. For instance, if you cast the love spell we discussed above, the one that is supposed to force a specific person to love you, you are binding that person. Binding is a magical problem that causes a backlash—a side-band.

You see, the Universe operates on the principle of reciprocal maintenance, which means that whatever you do to others will also happen to you. So if you bind another person with a love spell, you can be sure that you will find your own freedom bound in some way, against your will. The experience will *not* be pleasant!

SOME STORIES OF REAL WITCHCRAFT AND MAGIC

Sometimes nothing is as convincing as "real life" stories of witchcraft and magic. While we definitely want you to discover that the practice of these sciences can be real and effective in your own life through your own experience and observation, we also want to share with you some great stories. These stories will help ground the somewhat mystical concepts of magic and witchcraft into the framework of daily life. Plus, some of them are quite entertaining and we hope you will enjoy reading them!

THE GREAT DOG ESCAPE

The spells and rituals that I had recently learned in Basic Magic class came to the rescue recently in an adventure I call "The Great Dog Escape." Without magic, New Year's Eve 2001 could have meant Auld Lange Syne for me and Birgit, my Arctic white wolf/Akita cross, and her mate, Bjorn, the Chow Chow mix.

Birgit absolutely hates fireworks, so she tunneled out from under the six-foot chain link fence (with hot wire) during the festivities of the neighborhood, even though I had given her an herbal anxiety remedy. I returned from a potluck to find nothing but a hole under the fence and a tuft of wolf hair.

After searching frantically and calling the dogcatcher, I calmed down and began to use the "water bowl," a magical technique that I had recently learned (for finding lost objects and for telepathic communication). At first, I saw Birgit's head exploding, which I translated as bad news.

Over the next few days, I connected with the dogs and felt their life force, a great relief. Birgit let me know the firework explosions made her crazy in the head. Bjorn "said" he just went along for the ride, but he was now very sorry because he had something stuck between his eyes. Both communicated they didn't know how to get home. I told them we needed a third party to help us, because I didn't know where they were.

Four days after their departure, the two escapees were brought home by the dogcatcher. They had taken refuge in someone's doghouse, where they were found and reported. They came home tired, hungry, thirsty, and smelling strongly of skunk.

Birgit apologized in dog "body language," though she seemed relieved because I had assured her in the water bowl conversations that she wasn't in trouble. And Bjorn had a porcupine quill between his eyes, a real confirmation of the accuracy of the water bowl technique.

Using the water bowl to contact the dogs kept me from untold grief during the beginning of the New Year, a time I used to envision my goals for the rest of the year. Had I a bit more practice with the technique, I probably could have even found the dogs without the help of the family with the doghouse and the dogcatcher.

I plan to board the animals for New Year's Eve next year, but I am practicing the water bowl technique in case I ever need to help someone else.

— *Dawn*
Texas

HEALING A HAWK

Shortly after I began taking the Basic Magic class, my husband and I were driving down from the mountains back to town. As we drove on the highway, my husband saw a beautiful hawk sitting on a fence post. Just as he started to point it out to me, the hawk took off and flew head first at top speed into our windshield.

In the rear view mirror, my husband saw him land at the side of the road after being thrown over the top of the car. Our windshield was broken, including three large crack marks down the middle to attest to the force with which the hawk hit. We just knew he could not have survived the impact, but stopped anyway to see if we could do anything.

My husband found him at the side of the road and miraculously he was still alive, but something was terribly wrong with his left wing. It just hung uselessly, and looked like it was hardly attached anymore. He stumbled along the ground as my husband approached. The hawk was unable to fly away and looked seriously hurt.

I then remembered what I had learned in Basic Magic, and thought it couldn't hurt to try some energy work. I first gave the hawk some Sun Yellow energy, and then some Sky Blue Air and Clear Air. Suddenly the hawk took off just as I had finished my energy work, and we watched him soar, flap, and use that wing as if nothing had happened. We watched until he had totally flown out of sight and I was sure he would be fine.

— *Brita*
Texas

Communicating with Ghosts

I have a friend who is a very practical, grounded sort of guy. He does not believe in things he cannot see or explain to himself. Throughout my magic class however, he had to admit that what I was doing had merit, even though he could not understand it. I had done several healing techniques on him that had wonderful results that he could not deny.

Now in his house there was some type of Spirit in residence. It knocked things over, flushed toilets at night, and generally did all sorts of things we had always thought were along the lines of practical jokes. One day it moved a heavy dresser, which had previously taken four grown men to move, across the room. My friend finally admitted that he, too, believed there was something there—a Spirit or ghost.

He asked me if I could find out any information about it. Through pendulum work and Tarot readings, I was actually able to get quite a lot of information about why this Spirit was in this particular house, the name of the Spirit, some basic information about him, and what the "practical jokes" were really about.

I passed this information on to my friend. From that time on my friend began to talk to this entity by name and include it as part of the family. The "practical jokes" stopped, since the Spirit now had the attention it was trying to get.

One night my friend had fallen asleep with a heating pad on his sore shoulder. He dreamt of this Spirit—even hearing the Spirit's name in the dream. In the dream the

Spirit was telling him to wake up and put out a fire. It was such a vivid and real dream that my friend could actually feel the heat of the fire. He suddenly woke up and found that the heat he was feeling was not just in the dream. It was real. Something had malfunctioned with the heating pad, and it was smoking and beginning to burn him! In a state of half-sleep he turned the heating pad off, and thanked his Spirit friend for the warning.

However, he did not unplug the pad from the wall outlet. He returned to sleep with the heating pad now on the floor next to the bed. Again he dreamed of his Spirit friend trying to wake him up and leave because the house was aflame. He awoke to find that the heating pad was still smoking and had just started a flame on the carpet next to the bed. It could have easily turned into a house fire if his Spirit friend had not come to him in Dreamtime and awakened him.

— Luna
Colorado

BLOWING OFF STEAM SAFELY!

I had recently begun taking the Basic Magic class to learn new paradigms in my observation of "reality." I was hoping it would offer me more options and choices in my life.

One of the best techniques I learned was how to safely ground out Fire energy, which often manifests, for me, in the form of anger. One day, when I was nearing explosion in an argument with my wife, rather than continue on that path toward rage, I tried a magical technique to ground out anger.

I stretched out on the floor, put my bare feet on the stove/range, and flowed red/orange (anger) out of me and into the stove until I felt very different. Afterward, I felt much calmer. I was able to think, "Okay, I don't need to blow up in anger. There are lots of other choices." I did not escalate the fight any further.

The change was wonderful. It was a change as much in the energy as in the dialogue with my wife. My wife is really sensitive to energy. After I had flowed out the red/orange, she said, "OK, something is different." We ended up tabling the discussion for later instead of continuing the fight.

I was so glad that we learned to ground out anger by sending that energy into a major electrical appliance like the refrigerator or the stove/range. I did not actually feel the anger leave me, but suddenly I felt the *effect* of it leaving. At first, I was steaming mad, but the floor and range were cold. During the flowing process, suddenly I felt a sensation like, "Ahhhh…" and the anger left me.

If I told my friends about this experience, they would laugh so hard and ask me, "What planet are you from?" I really don't care! These magical practices work great!

— *Mike*
Colorado

3

WHAT IS A SPELL? WHAT IS A RITUAL?

Since this book is about witchcraft spells and rituals, we should definitely define the terms "spell" and "ritual" before diving into the actual procedures. That way you have a clear idea of what procedures you will learn later in this book, as well as their effects.

WHAT IS A SPELL?

A spell is any psychic or magical operation that combines a number of elements (Air, Fire, Water and Earth) and/or program factors that produce a particular result over a period of time.

A spell could also be defined as a formalized intention that is carried out over time until completion. We use spells when we are unable to directly affect a situation or condition, especially when dealing with complex factors or barriers which require a lot of force to overcome.

By the above definition, chants, litanies, rituals, and sonics are all spells. Prayers are also spells. Spells are energy matrices programmed to build momentum and overcome obstacles until the end goal is manifested. Unless otherwise programmed with directors and limiters (what the spell will and will not do), spells take the path of least resistance to the goal. While the goal may be appropriate relative to Rules of the Road, the path of the spell may be highly destructive (and not appropriate according to Rules of the Road).

The above is the *formal* definition of a spell. When you get right down to it, a spell is nothing more than a formalized intention supported by any powers and beings you might invite to help. A spell is the formalization of your own intention... your desire to create a specific effect in the world.

What is a Ritual?

A ritual, as defined above, is a form of a spell. In witchcraft and magic, rituals are usually simplified spells that are used frequently to make contact with higher powers and beings on a regular basis—these are called contact rituals. Contact rituals are especially important if you want to become a powerful practitioner who can ask for and receive aid and assistance from higher powers and beings, including Spirit guides, totem animals, angels, and the beings in the different directions of the Medicine Wheel.

Rituals are also used to deepen and re-affirm our own intentions, and that is the reason that they are performed more frequently than more formalized and complicated spells, such as candle or Tarot spells (both of which are quite advanced forms of witchcraft or magic).

WHAT IS THE DIFFERENCE BETWEEN A SPELL AND A RITUAL?

In magic and witchcraft, both spells and rituals are intentions that have been formalized into a series of specific actions meant to create particular effects in the world. For the most part, these effects would be considered "miraculous" by non-practitioners. In reality, these effects are simply what higher powers and beings consider "normal." Higher powers and beings—such as angels, animal totems, and Spirit guides—live on planes above our physical Earth plane, and the practice of miracles is simple for them, requiring no more effort than it takes us to heat up a cup of coffee!

Practically speaking, spells tend to be more complex, require much more effort to plan and perform, and are often performed fewer times (often only once). Rituals, on the other hand, are often much simpler. Practitioners often perform rituals more often, and many rituals are intended to be performed daily or even multiple times per day.

However, these are simply some practical definitions, and not all practitioners will agree on the differences in definition between spells and rituals. Here we simply offer you some definitions as "rules of thumb" to consider as you read through this book.

As with everything in this book, *nothing* should be taken on blind faith. Always remember, none of the information in this book should be taken as *true* until you have verified that information by ***your own direct observation and experience.*** This is *your* journey into the worlds of magic and witchcraft, and thus you must verify each step along the way for yourself—no exceptions!

USING SPELLS AND RITUALS TO SHIFT FROM THE MUNDANE TO THE MAGICAL

Did you know that the line between the magical and the mundane is so thin as to be practically invisible? You don't need to find and cross through the *Mists of Avalon* to live a magical life. You don't need to find the *Hogwarts School* to manifest the so-called "miracles" that are ordinary and normal to the witchcraft practitioner. Nope, you just need to take a single itty-bitty step using a single spell or ritual to cross that line. That's it. No exceptions. No lie. No kidding.

The fact of the matter is that most people simply get busy or forgetful... they forget to use even the simplest rituals or spells that they have learned. This is true not just of readers of our books, but even of our advanced students who have been studying with us for more than a decade!

So don't feel bad if you forget how to cross from the mundane into the witchy or magical. It happens to the most advanced practitioners, and is simply the result of the hypnotic effects of ordinary life. Just think about how often you are bombarded by cell phones, pagers, and requests to multi-task, not to mention the need to juggle the demands of work, family, health, and pleasure. That's a *lot* to handle… and that's what keeps us from remembering to use spells and rituals.

One of our favorite ways to remember to step back into the magical is this line from the song by the band Brewer & Shipley:

"One Step Over the Line, Sweet Jesus."

In reality, that line really goes, "One Toke Over the Line, Sweet Jesus," but you get the point... use whichever line works for you, so long as it reminds you to use a magical spell or ritual when you are having a bad hair day! This line is great because it speaks so eloquently about how little it takes to go from living a boring and often unbearably mundane life to a witchy, magical, miraculous life.

The difference is just one step. One itty-bitty step.

It doesn't matter whether you say Jesus or Universe or Great Spirit... you fill in the blank. The key is that the line between the mundane and the magical is a tiny one. It takes just one step to cross that line. Just one ritual. Just one simple spell. Just. One.

INTENTION MAKES ALL THE DIFFERENCE

Above, we defined spells and rituals as formalized intentions. So here's a kicker that might blow you right out of your shoes. In case you didn't make the connection before, here's a conclusion that comes naturally out of that definition:

Any intentional act is a magical act.

Stop and savor the power of that for a moment. *Any* intentional act is a magical act. That means that anything you do with intention (or *attention*) is a magical act. That means that anyone can do magic. There are no muggles. Everyone can do magic.

A simple ritual done with intention is a magical act. A power walk around the neighborhood driven by intention is a magical act. Taking a deep breath on purpose is a magical act. Are you starting to see how easy this can be?

WHAT ARE INTENTIONAL ACTS AND WHY

DO THEM?

So let's clarify. An intentional act is any act you do on purpose. A very simple act can be intentional, and hence an act of witchcraft and magic. Here's an example of an intentional act.

1. You look at a pen on your desk.
2. You decide to pick up the pen right now.
3. You pick up the pen immediately after you make the decision.

There, you have just done a magical act... and crossed the line from the ordinary world to the magical world. It's simple.

Of course, the scale of the intentional act dictates the level of its effect. A small intentional act will give you a little magical power boost... help you step over the line, so to speak. A stronger magical ritual will help you stay over the line. Even more powerful magic rituals done on a daily basis as part of magical practice will help you live a magical life, even as you move through your ordinary daily activities.

Get it? Got it? Good!

Other Forces of Witchcraft and Magic

Does a spell or ritual have power in and of itself? Yes. A spell has many source of power outside of your own desire and force, including:

- higher powers and beings that respond to magic
- the force of magical practitioners who have used the spell or ritual previously
- the power of sound, as found in litanies, chants, and drumming
- the strength of any keyed (programmed) magical tools used during the spell
- the force of symbols, which are doorways to actual sources of power

A Story about Spells on the World Level

Throughout this book, we will remind you time and time again that you need to follow the written spell and ritual procedures *exactly* because otherwise there could be repercussions you won't like. The spells and rituals in this book have been tested again and again over long periods of time, so we know they are safe to use, even for the beginner practitioner.

Here we share a story about what happens when spells and rituals are performed without very specific intentions being set. Hopefully this story will help give credence to the fact that "altered procedures produce altered results." In other words, if you don't follow the exact spell and ritual directions, your results could get a little crazy!

When a Spell Goes Wonky

Here's an instructive story about the reason for specifying your intention with spells and rituals very carefully. A person involved in a meditation group, which taught people to get what they wanted using white light, ran into some unexpected consequences. The meditation group taught people to put the thing they wanted to manifest on a bulletin board, and then sit there imagining what it would be like to have it.

A woman with a difficult life wanted to pay off her house and car, plus receive a reliable income. She took a picture of her mortgage and wrote "paid" on it. She did the same thing with the car loan documents, and then asked for $250,000 free and clear. When she was asked whether she was worried about how this manifestation would come about she replied that she was not.

Then, her husband who had been a very stable person, instead of going to work one day stopped at the liquor store to buy liquor, bought a gun, got drunk, and killed himself. The life insurance paid off the house and car, and gave the woman $250,000 free and clear. He was the weakest link in the chain so, by taking the path of least resistance, the spell worked through him.

Before using any spell or ritual you must be very clear that the procedure has been tested as safe. Otherwise you risk side-effects that you will not like... at all! Remember, the Universe doesn't care what you intend to do... just what you *actually* do. The practice of witchcraft and magic require precision, and, once again: "altered procedures produce altered results!"

4

Do You Have to be a Witch, Warlock, or Other Supernatural Being to Do Witchcraft?

NOPE. NO WAY. NEVER.

Magic is the right of every planetary citizen. You *are* a citizen of Planet Earth, in case you were wondering! Everyone has the power and ability to be a magician and to practice magic. Absolutely everyone! No qualifications, caveats, "maybes" or "buts"!

No need to name or qualify yourself as a witch, warlock, gremlin, or what-have-you. In fact, you will find that most experienced practitioners in the arts of magic or witchcraft don't give themselves names at all.

Such names or titles tend to interfere with a strong practice, and do nothing more than inflate the ego.

You have no need to whip out a giant genealogical scroll that "verifies" your magical lineage. Nope, everyone *can* be a practitioner of witchcraft and magic. Every single person can experience magic in their lives, live a witchy life. There is no distinction between the "muggle" and the "magical." That's literally hogwash!

Magic and witchcraft are both art and science, with real rules, logic, and reasoning. These practices can be learned just as any science can be learned. You can start anytime, including today, right now! In fact, we encourage you to do just that.

A Little on the History of Witchcraft and Magic

For well over a million years, our ancestors roamed this planet and lived successfully—for the most part well—without needing all the aids and protections we have come to believe are necessary (think guns, toilets, or any other modern convenience that you believe you absolutely can't live without). Somehow, these Old Ones were able to balance themselves so as to harmonize with the requirements of life under a wide variety of conditions.

Magic and witchcraft are among the oldest sciences on our planet, their development beginning in the dim mists of the past when some ancient man undertook willful contact with higher powers, and manipulation of the physical environment by indirect and non-physical means.

Many of the ancients revered by our culture as "creators" of modern science were actually practitioners of magic and witchcraft whose research happened to develop in culturally acceptable ways. The same is true of the ancients, now regarded as great philosophers or teachers, who were practitioners whose research uncovered basic knowledge about the non-physical aspects of the Universe.

So it is that these spiritual practices can be seen as a science, and studied and practiced as such, either within or outside of a religious framework. Though the technical language of magic and witchcraft is different from that of the modern scientist, the practitioner works with the same laws and principles of the Universe as the physicist, chemist, or astronomer.

The competent practitioner uses the laws from a slightly different viewpoint and in slightly different ways, whether to heal the sick, avert a disaster, divine the past or future, or perform rituals of invocation or banishment of non-physical beings.

The major difference between the physical scientist and the spiritual practitioner is that the former uses the psyche, mind, and body to build physical tools to manipulate the Universe. The latter considers the psyche, mind, and body to *be* the tools, occasionally using additional tools to refine their control.

Magical effects, such as telepathy, clairvoyance, telekinesis, psychic healing, spells, and prayers are merely particular applications of the laws and principles governing electricity, internal-combustion engines, or chemical reactions.

The practitioner understands the Universe in terms of four basic elements: Air, Fire, Water, and Earth. Thoughts, emotions, chemicals, experiences, bodies, and even atomic and sub-atomic physics can be successfully analyzed and understood with these four elements.

Because they lived in a completely different era, the "creators" of magic and witchcraft had the awareness and balancing skills (in terms of energy handling) that we of 21st century America do not have. We must devote much time and work in studies, such as those in this book, to develop the same skills that came naturally to the Old Ones. We modern planetary citizens must work hard to overcome the sluggishness and hypnosis of today's society.

We hope that in working with this material you will become a happier, healthier, and more "evolved" human as a result of your efforts.

We, the authors of this book, can do magic and so can you. We practice the spells and rituals of magic and witchcraft daily. So can you. We are no different. We have a few more years of experience than you, but we started out as baby spell-casters, too. It is simpler than you might think. You can start out taking baby steps by doing small rituals and grow your magical practice from there.

5

Why Develop a Regular Witchcraft or Magical Practice?

We discussed the power of a witchcraft or magical practice earlier in this book. We talked about how running your own experiment by doing a simple ritual or spell for 40 days in a row can help you establish whether you should have faith in these practices. We also outlined the power of this kind of spiritual practice—that whatever you put into your 40-day experiment (a short version of a regular practice) will eventually pay you back.

Here, we just want to add a short note on the power of a regular, daily practice based on the spells and rituals outlined in this book. Becoming a regular practitioner of witchcraft and magic can make a very powerful change in your life in quite a short period of time.

In fact, some people believe in this principle so strongly that they have become ***slaves to their practices***. This sounds kind of extreme, but it's actually a very common principle in many esoteric and tribal practices. The gist of it is this: according to most spiritual practices, there can only be one "most important" thing in your life. That *one thing* will either be your intentional spiritual practice or it will be ordinary life, which is filled with accidental events not controlled by intention.

In many magical traditions, students are instructed to choose an aim (or ritual) and to make that aim their singular focus in life. Why? Because the aim or ritual is intentional, which means it creates a very precise and pre-determined desired effect.

Just as importantly, that effect acts as an antidote against all the "accidents" that otherwise occur in life: the fender-benders, the sick kids, the job layoff, the life-threatening health diagnosis, and other calamities. So being a slave to your chosen spiritual practice simply means putting more attention on that practice than on ordinary life. It means putting your practice first, even when you think you are too tired, too stressed, too [*you fill in the blank...*]!

HOW A REGULAR PRACTICE LOOKS IN DAILY LIFE

Here's how it would work. Suppose you choose the magic ritual of hiring an angel every single day as your regular ritual practice. Now suppose you get into a fender bender. What do you do?

1. Don't panic. Just mutter a couple of curse words under your breath if that makes you feel better!
2. Whip out your chosen ritual, which is to hire an angel. Hire an angel to fix this mess (before you even get out of the car to deal with the other driver).
3. Get out of your car and deal with whatever practical life issues need to be handled, such as trading insurance information.

Notice how this sequence of actions puts your chosen ritual first, and then takes care of practical world-plane issues. By putting your magic ritual ahead of acts on the physical plane, you attract more magic and intention, and fewer accidents. We assume, of course, that the fender bender is minor and you have 15 seconds to hire an angel before hopping out of the car. If not, use common sense and take care of business first and hire an angel later. Just remember to put your emphasis on the idea that your spiritual practice is more important than panicking about the life situation... then you'll be golden (and witchy)!

6

Rules of the Road

Universal Laws for Any Practitioner of Witchcraft or Magic

Thanks to Reverend George Dew of the Church of Seven Arrows for researching and putting these rules together. While similar to the Wiccan Rede, we feel these Universal laws are stated more practically and pragmatically for everyday use.

Rules of the Road are Universal laws, but this can still be confusing. Go to enough magical and witchcraft seminars, and you may start to wonder which rules are "true" and which ones are not.

At one seminar you may learn that you can't use magic or witchcraft for personal gain. At another workshop they teach you to use daily rituals for nothing *but* personal gain.

So who is right? Which set of Universal laws should you follow?

It is a confusing situation to be sure, but rest assured that the ***Rules of the Road*** specified here are Universal laws that *do* govern the practice of witchcraft and magic. We have verified that these laws effectively work according to our own experience and observation.

RULES OF THE ROAD

Rules of the Road are the set of Universal ethics, which must be followed for safe and effective magical practice. The Rules of the Road are not the same as morals (what our culture teaches us is right and wrong) or ethics (what we personally believe to be right and wrong), since both morals and ethics change over time. Particular or personal morals or ethics may or may not agree with the Rules of the Road.

The Universe does not recognize morals and ethics because they vary from culture to culture, and they change over time. Experienced practitioners use the Rules of the Road defined here to guide them in their practices instead of relying on their own personal value systems.

To practice magic safely and effectively you must know and abide by the Rules of the Road since, as far as we know, the Rules of the Road operate whether you know of them, believe in them, or agree with them or not—like the law of gravity in the earlier example. Additionally, normal scientific physical laws and principles must be followed.

AS USUAL, DON'T JUST TAKE OUR WORD FOR IT

George Dew gave us this set of Universal laws, and we have "put the rubber to the road" in our own practices to ensure that they actually work. We can assure you that our experience shows that these Universal laws are effective, useful, and true.

But that is not good enough. As a practitioner of witchcraft or magic, you need to verify for yourself whether these Universal laws are going to work for you and your practice. Never take our word for it. Try out these Universal laws.

As mentioned earlier in this book, you can consider your own experience of anything described in this book as a magical experiment. Just be sure to record your results carefully, since your memory is not as accurate as you think it might be! After that, you can decide whether these Universal laws are ones that you want to follow.

TWO MAJOR RULES:

1. **Whatever is done to the environment or to other beings in the environment brings similar effects upon the doer.**

   This is often called the Law of Karma. The Universe does not care why some action was taken, or whether the doer is trained in magic or aware of the Rules of the Road. Although many different teachers have stated this law in many different ways, including calling this law the Golden Rule, this law is especially important for practitioners of witchcraft and magic. This means that a practitioner's acts are consciously and willfully directed—thus, much more focused—and are therefore more powerful than the acts of untrained people. So the effect of this law in relation to a practitioner's acts becomes much more powerful. This applies to both constructive and destructive acts.

Note: WHILE MANY RELIGIOUS AND OTHER PRACTICES CONSIDER THAT KARMA CAN CARRY FROM LIFETIME TO LIFETIME, IT IS OUR EXPERIENCE THAT THE UNIVERSE OPERATES UNDER A SYSTEM OF "PAY AS YOU GO." IN OTHER WORDS, THE EFFECT OF ANY ACT UPON THE ENVIRONMENT (OR UPON BEINGS IN THE ENVIRONMENT) COMES BACK TO YOU WITHIN A RELATIVELY SHORT PERIOD OF TIME—OFTEN WITHIN HOURS OR DAYS.

2. **The magician judges the "goodness" or "badness" of his or her own acts, whether they are conscious or unconscious acts, on the basis of what the Universe reflects back on him or her. The same is true of judging others, entire communities, states, or nations.**

   On a practical level, one can judge one's compliance with the Universe's standards of right and wrong, or good and bad, in terms of one's level of health, soundness of social relationships, luck with appliances, and sufficiency of food, clothing and shelter. If your "luck" seems consistently bad, then you're probably acting contrary in some way to the Rules of the Road, regardless of what your intentions are.

ETHICAL LAWS OF THE RULES OF THE ROAD

These ethical laws will give you a more detailed standard by which to measure your acts, or the acts of others, to determine whether they are in accordance with Rules of the Road. Judge any act of magic or witchcraft by these laws before doing it.

1. Do nothing that will harm another being unless you are willing to suffer like or greater harm. Note that what the Universe considers harm may be different from what our culture teaches as harm.

2. Do not bind another being unless you are willing to be likewise bound. This applies to many love spells and some kinds of healing rituals.

3. Never use magic for show, pride, or vainglory. Using magic to show off, to prove a point, or from a place of injured pride usually results in side-bands (undesirable side effects) to the operation that will bring very undesirable backlash from the Universe.

4. Never set an extremely high price for the use of magic (especially divination, healing, or spells) based on your having special knowledge. With some operations that take significant man hours, such as divination, it appears by our observation to be appropriate to charge the same fee as any other professional might charge per hour in your local area.

5. Do not use any special word, symbol, incantation, or spell unless you understand thoroughly and

completely its mechanics, content, and intent! Be very wary of using other people's operations if you wish to avoid "frying" yourself, either figuratively or literally!

6. Never do a spell without first doing a divination to determine a) if you should do it, and b) exactly what needs to be dealt with. Modern American social values and overt appearances of a situation are not trustworthy guides for a practitioner wishing to avoid bad karma. In other words, there may be hidden factors in the situation, which cause the doing of a spell to be against Rules of the Road.
7. **Take your time, think it through, and do it right!**

LOOK UP ANYTHING YOU DON'T UNDERSTAND

As an addendum to the Rules of the Road, another helpful principle is to look up any word in this book that you don't understand. If "altered procedures produce altered results" is true, then working with words that you do not understand, for instance, could very well lead to altered results!

You may need to buy yourself a good dictionary to help you with the spells and rituals outlined in this book. Take the first definition offered because in American English, new words are not added to the language so much as the meanings of existing words are changed. The original definition is usually listed first, so to get the original meaning of a word, take the first definition.

FOLLOW DIRECTIONS EXACTLY AS GIVEN!

Did you know that the practitioner of magic and witchcraft has a very different view of the Universe than the average man or woman on the street? By now this should not surprise you. To the spiritual practitioner the Universe is orderly, full of never-ending wonder, and neither particularly hostile nor particularly friendly, except insofar as whether it is approached correctly or not.

Approached incorrectly, the Universe, like any other machine, can become a thing fraught with fate, luck, and other "untold awful mysteries" lurking in wait at every turn.

If, on the other hand, it is approached correctly, the Universe becomes a thing of consummate interest and enlightenment, a place where one can learn and grow and enjoy unendingly, each turn of the path bringing some new wonder into view for joyful exploration. In other words, the Universe becomes a place of miracles and magic!

THE SAFE AND SUCCESSFUL USE OF THE PROCEDURES GIVEN IN THIS COURSE REQUIRES TWO THINGS FROM YOU:

1. Careful and detailed reading of the text materials (look up all words you don't understand in a good dictionary, being careful to use the first meaning given as the original meaning of the word).
2. Following precisely the instructions given for any particular exercise or operation. Remember that "***altered procedures produce altered results***"!

A QUICK NOTE ABOUT "PERSONAL GAIN"

Many people worry about whether rituals of magic and witchcraft can be used for personal gain or whether there will be backlash. Just watch a couple episodes of the popular TV series "Charmed" and you might be convinced that you can *never* use these spells and rituals for personal gain.

Not so.

The whole myth that you can't do magic or witchcraft for personal gain is bogus. If you can't use these spells and rituals as a recourse in a life that is admittedly unfair at times, what is it for?

The spells and rituals taught in this and other books in this series *can and should* be used to improve your life. Many practitioners have used these spells and rituals to attract money, recognition, and other life conditions, all without backlash.

Can you use magic or witchcraft to win the lottery? You can try, but it probably won't work. Why not? Because the general thought forms from the majority of people in society is strongly against winning. Most people buy lottery tickets "expecting" not to win. This is a topic for a whole other book, but know that Rules of the Road, the Universal laws that govern practitioners, do not prohibit the use of magic for personal gain.

So go ahead, practice witchcraft and magic, and gain!

7

THE INCONVENIENCE FACTOR AND MAGICAL BUDDIES

WHAT IS THE "INCONVENIENCE FACTOR"?

It has been our observation, through the teaching of many classes, that the student of magic and witchcraft inevitably comes up against the "inconvenience factor" when beginning to study this material. In other words, at some point early in your training, it is likely that taking the time to do your rituals and spells will be highly inconvenient. The inconvenience factor will require you to make many small and some radical changes in your life to make room in your life for this new spiritual practice.

For some people, the inconvenience factor manifests in the inability to study because of a sudden bout of phone calls, relatives unexpectedly coming to visit, work hours becoming radically increased, or unexpected travel. For others, family or career demands suddenly become "too much" and "something must give." For others, some drastic event occurs in their life.

All those who have pushed through the inconvenience factor and stayed the course have found their lives radically improved, no matter the temporarily inconvenient conditions in which they find themselves.

You will have to make the choice of which is more important—your new spiritual practice or convenience. In making your choice, remember this: while the practice of magic and witchcraft may be highly inconvenient in the beginning, when applied properly, it can greatly reduce the level of struggle and increase the level of joy in your life in the long run.

At the beginning of your journey as a practitioner you will be able to straddle the two worlds, mundane and magical, sometimes choosing mundane convenience and other times choosing your practice. However, as you progress in your studies, your intention will tend to grow in strength and force. The result is that the two worlds will diverge more and more. At some point, you will need to make a choice between the two worlds—magical or mundane? You will know when you have reached that point... and then it will be up to you to make your decision.

We want to leave you with one final note on your decision regarding the inconvenience factor. Based on the experience of teaching students over the last 30 years, we have found that for almost every student there is a specific "window of opportunity" during which a spiritual practice is most easily integrated into daily life. The inconvenience factor continues to be present, but when a student chooses to forge ahead with his or her spiritual studies, the inconvenience factor tends to disappear more quickly.

Those students who choose the convenience of ordinary life—no doubt thinking that they will return to the development of their spiritual practice later—find that when they try to return to their spiritual practice, the "window of opportunity" is closed. While it is still possible for these students to develop a spiritual practice, the resistance is much greater than before.

As a word to the wise, when you come to the point at which you need to make a decision about whether to move forward with your spiritual practice or attend to mundane life issues, think about the "window of opportunity" before you make your choice.

WHY HAVING A BUDDY HELPS WITH YOUR SPIRITUAL PRACTICE

Having taught hundreds of students over the last 30 years, we have observed that students who undertake the study of magic or witchcraft with friends, partners, or significant others generally have much better results.

Therefore, before you commence to build your spiritual practice we suggest that you attempt to find a "buddy" to work with. A buddy can help you stay on track, remind you of the inconvenience factor, and trade experiences with you (especially when you feel that the rituals or spells "are not working").

Your buddy can also help you "see" some effects of magic or witchcraft in your life. We all have blind spots, and buddies can help us see through them. For instance, many people can see when something "good" happens in their lives, but fail to see when a negative influence has left their lives.

For instance, we often counsel people about health care. We often ask them to tell us if anything has changed or improved with their health after we have completed a treatment regimen. Many times the person says, "No, nothing has changed." But when we ask them whether they still have headaches or back pain, they suddenly become aware of the fact that the pain is gone. We often fail to notice when pain leaves our lives. Pain or negative events are usually noticeable only when they are present. So be sure to have your buddy help you check for anything negative that might have left your life.

It is easy, especially in the beginning of a spiritual practice, to become overwhelmed with the daily tasks of life and forget to do your spells and rituals. Having one or more partners to check with throughout the week will help you remember that you are a practitioner engaged in paying into your spiritual practice. Plus, having partners makes this study much more engaging and fun!

8

WHY YOU NEED YOUR OWN PERSONAL BOOK OF SHADOWS

A lot of people wonder, "What is a book of shadows? Is it fact or fiction?" In fact, many thousands of people type the search term "real book of shadows" into online search engines every month to try to find out.

If you watch the TV show "Charmed" then you'll know that the Halliwell sisters have a giant book of spells written by their ancestors called a book of shadows. Others will take a hint from the title of the second "Blair Witch" movie, despite there being no actual book in the movie. Still others think a book of shadows is something like a personal journal for Wiccans, an idea popularized by Gerald Gardner, who brought Wiccan practices to public attention with his book "Witchcraft Today," published in 1954.

Why You Need Your Own Personal Book of Shadows

Obviously the definition of a real book of shadows varies widely in popular culture, among magical and witchcraft practitioners as well, depending on which tradition they practice. However, most practitioners agree on three common usages and purposes for a real book of shadows, which we discuss below.

> ***We strongly suggest that you get a book of shadows (or more than one book) before you begin practicing the spells and rituals described in this book.***

A well-recorded book of shadows will aid your memory, help you track your progress, and be of immense use should you need to take down a spell that has gone awry!

1. Record Spell Details

A book of shadows is used to record all the details of spells cast. For spells in particular, items recorded in the book of shadows may include any divinations done prior to a spell, the directors and limiters for a spell (what you intend the spell to do *and* not do), methods used, results of divinations to check spell progress, and any results of the spell.

Having all these details recorded is especially important if you need to take a spell down because of something going wrong. The way a spell is taken down depends on the way it was cast. For example, if the spell was cast using a carved candle then to take it down the practitioner could break the candle used in the spell and bury the pieces in a garden for a moon cycle.

2. Track Magical and Shamanic Research

Magical and witchcraft practitioners often engage in research, such as discovering facts about past lives, divining future events, trying out new techniques, or traveling to different planes.

In the traditions of the Esoteric School of Shamanism and Magic, we record the results of walks in the black mirror, a portal to other planes of existence or half-worlds. When we do these walks we use a litany or chant to direct the walk and to keep from getting lost. Recording details about the walk upon returning adds to our body of magical knowledge, and also records the effectiveness of the chant so it can be used again or fine-tuned for future use.

Other items that we record in our book of shadows include rituals performed, divinations conducted, observations noted, witchcraft experiments (with all the necessary safety precautions, of course), blessings offered... in short, all magical or witchcraft procedures.

3. Preserve Magic and Witchcraft for the Future

Preserving knowledge of magic and witchcraft for future practitioners is one of the most important purposes of a book of shadows. Most traditions recognize the importance of information and practices passed on from past practitioners. Your personal book of shadows can contain the research and results of multiple generations of practitioners handed down through the years. Each generation of practitioners, not necessarily related, adds their experience to the book.

A book of shadows is a record of the practitioner's experience that is preserved either for a practitioner's own use or for future use. Note that some practitioners keep individual books and never hand them down for their own personal reasons.

However, we recommend that all practitioners keep one or more books of shadows. A book of shadows will help you remember what you have done, track your magical experiments, and possibly be an asset for the future. We suggest that you keep a separate book of shadows each for spells and rituals, divination, general observations, and experiments.

One important reason to keep multiple books of shadows is that you should always keep your book of shadows dedicated to spell work locked and safe at home—spells are specific forms of practice that you do not want random strangers reading. On the other hand, you may need to carry your book of shadows dedicated to divination outside the home, to do Tarot readings and such. There is much less danger associated with other people reading through your divination book of shadows.

Protecting Your Book of Shadows

Many traditions suggest that you place symbols on the front and back of your book of shadows, either for decoration or more likely for protection. These can range from very simple to very intricate.

Shield (old symbol)

Disc (current symbol)

In the Esoteric School of Shamanism and Magic, we protect our books of shadows with the magical symbol for the Plate or Pantacle, also called the Disc in the Tarot (see images of Shield and Disc provided). The Disc is preferable to the Shield symbol, being more appropriate to the modern age. This symbol, drawn on the front and back of a book of shadows, locks and protects the book physically and psychically. In addition, use your common sense to keep your books of shadows in a hidden place not easily accessible to visitors to your home.

9
Beginner Rituals and Spells

Rituals and Spells Done With Your Bare Hands

9.1

Beginner Rituals and Spells

Contact Rituals for Sky and Earth

Hallelujah!

You are about to learn your very first witchcraft ritual in this book! This ritual is what we call a "contact ritual," and is the first of three forms of the Navajo Beauty Way (although this ritual was a tribal tradition long before the Navajos ever used it). This form is called the Exit Ritual.

The Exit Ritual is a contact and greeting ritual that reconnects us to powers and beings. People call powers and beings by all kinds of different names: Universe, God, Higher Power, Angels, Totem Spirits, etc. It doesn't matter what view you take, just know that there are higher beings that exist all around who cannot wait to help you out!

Connecting with powers and beings is useful because they can help you get back into that feeling of peace and serenity. They exist at a higher level than we do, so it's often easier to ask them for help rather than trying to "do it all" ourselves. The Exit Ritual also realigns our chi or life force, which can become distorted from working and living in buildings with strong electromagnetic fields.

HOW TO DO THE EXIT RITUAL

To do the Exit Ritual, follow this procedure every time you leave an enclosed space such as a car, building or house:

1. Extend your focus up into the sky and say aloud, "Sky Above." The reason we extend our focus first is that the Exit Ritual is a form of making contact with and asking favor from powers and beings. Thus it is appropriate that we go to them (with our focus) rather than asking them to come to us.

   In ritual, we only invite powers and beings to come to us after we have carefully prepared an appropriate sacred space for them. Once we have completed the ritual, we then thank them, and then bid them farewell. Because we don't want to go to all that trouble, in this case we simply extend our focus first, and then make contact.

2. While keeping your awareness above, extend your focus into the Earth and say aloud, "And Earth Below."

3. Then, keeping awareness of both above and below, say aloud, "I Greet You."

4. Wait a moment and see what happens. Be alert for acknowledgement or response in one of these three ways:

   - from within you, such as a realization, a change of attitude or belief, a new awareness

   - changes in your environment, such as a sudden breeze, a change in the color of the sky, a bird or animal suddenly appearing visually or vocally, or a tree or shrub suddenly becoming vividly visible

   - a response from Sky and/or Earth: a special message for you, an answer to a question, or guidance and new directions. Note that this message may sound like a voice in your own mind. This is perfectly normal. What will be different is that the message will usually be different than what you say to yourself

5. What happens may happen in just that moment, or it may happen throughout the day. It may change the quality of your day, your awareness... whatever you notice. You may also want to use arm gestures. Arms raised in a upward facing V for "Sky Above" and arms down in a downward facing V for "Earth Below."

THE BENEFITS OF THE EXIT RITUAL

The Navajo Beauty Way Exit Ritual is a quick and easy way to get reconnected with your inner peace and serenity. Deep inside, you are always peaceful, happy, and serene. It is just that sometimes you just may not remember how to access that part of yourself.

The Navajos used several forms of the Beauty Way to help them stay connected with their cultural identity when they were being moved onto reservations. While the Navajos are not the first tribe to use the Beauty Way, they are among the recent tribes to make use of this basic spell. Ancient tribes who roamed the Earth eons ago also made use of all three forms of the Beauty Way, under different names but in essentially the same form.

This ritual is a non-denominational set of exercises from very ancient times, which has many spiritual purposes. This ritual can:

- restore personal power
- develop a practical working relationship with higher powers and beings or natural forces and laws
- be safe and protected without the need to build walls or hide behind masks
- maintain spiritual integrity for individuals or groups during times of high external change and stress.

One additional benefit of doing this ritual is the health

benefit. We are constantly surrounded by electromagnetic fields that emanate from computers, TVs, radios, microwaves and the electrical grid that power our homes and offices. These electromagnetic fields disturb our life force on a daily basis, leading to all kinds of health issues. The Exit Ritual, because it causes us to extend our energies both up and down, realigns our life force and chi, restoring healthy balance to our energies. We find that the Exit Ritual usually works better than aspirin for all kinds of ailments in body, mind, and Spirit!

> ***"The Exit Ritual is an incredible ritual that keeps me connected to heaven and earth. Whenever I'm having a bad day, I can go out and do the ritual to restart my day. It helps me remember that I'm a human being, not a human doing." - B. H.***

REMEMBERING TO THE DO THIS RITUAL

Remembering to do the Exit Ritual can be the one of the hardest parts of this beautiful ritual of contact with powers and beings. Benjamin Franklin said that it took at least 21 days to form a new habit. Many spiritual teachings emphasize 40 days as the amount of time needed to imbed something into your experience. So, if you are feeling frustrated by your own forgetfulness, take a breath and relax. We all forget to do rituals the beginning.

To help yourself remember, you might buy a pack of sticky

notes and post reminders to yourself on your doors (so that you see them as you go outside) and on the rearview mirror of your car. These will prompt you to remember. Alternately, program your smart phone to remind you.

Also, if you find yourself driving in your car and realize that you have forgotten to do the Exit Ritual, pull your car over to the side of the road and stop. Take the time, then and there, to get out of your car and do it. Once you have to stop your car a few times you'll begin to remember!

Good luck and keep up the effort—the rewards are worth all the effort! Here's the Exit Ritual again, compressed into four short lines to make it easier to remember:

Sky Above [extend attention into sky]

And Earth Below [extend attention into earth, keeping it in sky also]

I Greet You. [keep attention in both sky and earth]

[Pause a minute after saying this]

"I am amazed at the powerful pull I felt from the sky and the earth as I did this exercise. I have never felt that kind of power before. I don't have a clue what it means, but I can't wait to practice this ritual some more. I have tried many spiritual rituals, but this is by far the most real response I have received." - Sandy S.

OVERCOMING THE EMBARRASSMENT FACTOR

The embarrassment factor... we all have it. Do you find yourself embarrassed to do the Exit Ritual when you are in public? Are you afraid that people will think you are strange if you pause in a grocery store parking lot and appear to be talking to no one? Most of us have felt this kind of embarrassment at some point or other when starting to do this ritual.

Chances are, though, that most people are so busy hurrying through their day and buried in their own thoughts that they won't even notice what you are doing. However, if you do feel embarrassed, here are a few things you can do to make this ritual easier.

SUBVOCALIZE THE GREETING

You can still say the greeting, but speak it softly and quietly so that no one else can hear it. It is important that you speak the greeting aloud, but you can say it so quietly that only you will hear it.

KEEP YOUR EYES OPEN AND LOOK AHEAD

The instructions for the ritual say to extend your awareness or attention into the sky and earth. However, this does not mean that you have to look up or down. If you feel more comfortable, just keep your eyes open and looking naturally ahead while you do the greeting. Only extend your attention up and down, not your gaze. You will appear as if you are just stopping to remember something, such as a shopping list you might have left in your car.

START IN PRIVATE

If you feel uncomfortable doing the ritual when you are with other people or in public, start by doing it where you feel comfortable, then gradually step outside your comfort zone. Even if someone does stare at you or think you are strange, looks can't kill. Stepping outside your comfort zone with the Exit Ritual will help you be more comfortable taking risks in all other areas of your life.

Remember, you are not alone. There are hundreds of people all over the world doing this ritual, learning to get over their embarrassment, and getting all the gifts that come with this ritual. Keep going!

Why Consistently Doing This Ritual Lets You Ask for Favors Later!

Remember that with the Exit Ritual, you are greeting the Sky and the Earth. What happens when you greet a person on a regular basis in a friendly and caring way? You develop a relationship! That is exactly what you are doing here. You are developing a working relationship with the Sky and Earth.

Why would you want to develop a relationship with these powers? Because they can be incredible allies for any life situations in which you need a higher source of help. Once you have developed a deeper relationship with Earth and Sky, you can begin to ask for their help. You can ask them to help you find a new job, get more income, find a life partner, or restore your peace of mind. You can also get specific answers or guidance from these higher powers by asking them one or more questions after you have completed the ritual.

There is an esoteric law that states that we can rarely fully solve our own problems by ourselves. The truth is that it is much easier to seek help from deities or higher beings, who are able to handle these issues much more easily at their own level of existence.

It is tempting in our busy lives to skip this ritual because it can seem inconvenient when we are in a hurry, but when you look at the long term benefits of being consistent and developing a working relationship with sky and earth, it makes the ritual easier to do on a regular basis.

Hopefully, now that you understand that you are really communicating personally with live beings who can and want to help you in your daily life, the Exit Ritual won't be just another item on a to do list. It becomes more of a live, daily interaction with good friends!

HAVING A BAD HAIR DAY? THE EXIT RITUAL CAN HELP!

We all have those days when we get up on the wrong side of the bed, and the whole day just plummets downhill from there. On days like these, it seems like nothing goes right, no matter how hard we try. How frustrating!

Well, guess what? There *is* something you can do. You can start your day over with the Exit Ritual. If you find yourself having a bad day, take five minutes to walk outside and do the Exit Ritual. Then just stand there for a minute or two and let the peace and serenity of the moment wash over and through you.

Sky and Earth, with the vastness of their being and presence, will gift you with sudden peace and the start of a whole new day. For them, our entire day, all 24 hours of it, is simply a single breath. When we ask them to help us start our day over, it is nothing more than the equivalent of asking them to just take another breath. Not a big deal at all!

You can also do the Exit Ritual after any traumatic or stressful situation. It will literally help you get your feet back on the ground. You will get radiance and joy from the Sky, and solidity and strength from the Earth.

If you are with a bunch of people and don't want to be obvious, you can act like you are taking a moment to stop and tie your shoe. You don't have to be standing to do the ritual. Just extend your awareness into Sky and Earth. Have fun using this ritual, and watch how bad days magically transform into great ones!

GATHERING YOUR ALLIES WITH THE EXIT RITUAL

Once you have been doing the Exit Ritual for a while, notice whether you feel the difference that it can make in your life. If you don't believe your senses or if you feel doubt creeping in about your experience, do a little experiment and see for yourself. Stop doing the Exit Ritual for seven days and see what life is like. Then start doing the ritual again for seven days on a very consistent basis. See if you can feel the difference between the two experiences. Take notes morning and night rather than simply trusting your memory.

One of the key aspects to gain from your experience with the Exit Ritual is that you are not alone and are not expected to make a success out of life by yourself. Sky and Earth stand ready to help you whenever you ask. But, you have to take the time to develop a working and harmonious relationship with them.

Sky and Earth are never offended when you feel too busy or embarrassed to greet them. They wait patiently for you, watching your personal growth and development. When you finally do see what potent allies they are for you, they are ready to help. The door is always open with these beings, so don't feel bad if you haven't reached the point yet where you can greet them on a consistent basis. Just keep working on it. In fact, if you really want to see the power of their help, ask them to help you remember to do the ritual and to get over your embarrassment about doing it!

However much or little you choose to make use of this ritual, just remember that it is there for you whenever you need a little magic in your life. Most importantly, have fun with this witchy ritual and enjoy!

9.2

BEGINNER RITUALS AND SPELLS

HIRING PARKING AND OTHER UNEMPLOYED ANGELS

The news is full of stories on the increased unemployment rate in the United States. The news is filled with gloom and doom such as the following:

- predictions on the length of time required for the economy to recover
- the number of people who will file bankruptcy because of unemployment
- the need for unemployment benefit reform
- the percentage of Americans unable to make mortgage payments due to job loss

- whether the unemployment rate will go up or down
- and so much more about unemployment

These are difficult times for the human race, and the news media can't seem to stop reporting on *all aspects of unemployment.*

In actuality, we should say that the media reports on all aspects of unemployment *that they know about!* There is another population that suffers from high unemployment, and this is a group that is *never* mentioned by the news media.

Who are these unemployed beings? ANGELS!

That's right, we said angels. For much of Earth's history, angels have suffered from unemployment rates that make our current U.S. human unemployment rate look paltry. Especially in today's modern world, when belief in witchcraft and magic are low, angels are also finding themselves hanging around in unemployment lines. In these modern times, fewer and fewer people ask angels for help on a regular basis.

> ***Hopefully, with this ritual you will help angels improve their employment rate…not to mention improve your own life at the same time!***

It is so easy for humans to get caught up in their busy lives, their woes, stresses, and problems and completely forget, if indeed they ever knew, that angels are helpful resources. Angels are delighted to help us, virtually free of charge. There are angels whose expertise range in everything from travel to communication to health. So many things that are everyday irritants can be resolved by angels... we just have to remember to ask them for help.

HOW CAN ANGELS HELP US?

There is an angel out there for every single need. No kidding. Every need.

Are you running late for an appointment and want to make sure you have a parking place waiting for you? Hire an angel to pick out and save the perfect parking space for you. What if you are taking a driving trip, and want to make sure you arrive safely and on time? Hire a travel angel to keep you, your vehicle, and your belongings safe for the duration of your trip.

Suppose you have to resolve a misunderstanding with your boss, and you seriously dread having that conversation. Rather than sweating bullets, you could hire a communications angel to accompany you to the meeting with your boss to ensure smooth communication and deep understanding. Can't sleep at night? Hire a sleep angel to snooze peacefully. Are you starting to panic because you have taken on too heavy of a workload? Hire a productivity angel and be amazed at your own creativity and efficiency.

One reason that angels are so eager to help—aside from the fact that one of their main jobs is to help humans—is that they cannot evolve unless they help us. Because of Earth's Prime Directive, which is that no higher being can help humans unless directly asked, angels cannot offer us assistance unless we specifically ask them. So there are groups of angels just waiting, begging, for us to ask. So if you want to be of service while being served, hire an angel. It's both good for you and good for the angel!

Get the picture? Whenever you need help, just hire an angel. The ritual to hire an angel is very simple. To get you started, we'll teach you how to hire a parking space angel. After all, wouldn't it be sweet to find the perfect parking space everywhere you go with the help of a parking angel? Totally.

Once you master this ritual, you can expand your repertoire to include hiring angels for anything and everything. The possibilities are limitless...not to mention the fact that you will make so many angels very happy!

HOW TO HIRE A PARKING ANGEL

A great area in your life to practice hiring angels is to start with parking angels... in other words, angels who help you locate open and convenient parking spaces wherever you go! Try this little exercise of hiring a parking angel to help you find the perfect parking spot in any parking lot, busy or not.

1. Say out loud or in your mind, "I would like to a request a parking angel of Sun Yellow, Grass Green, and Sky Blue." (These are spiritual colors that are particularly attractive and useful to angels.)

2. Wait a few moments until you feel the angel's presence, or, just wait a few moments. Angels don't take long to arrive.

   Do not overthink this step. Angels *always* show up. If you are unsure as to whether you "feel" the presence of your requested angel, just wait 10 seconds or so, then move on to the next step. Don't worry, the angel will be waiting for your request.

3. Say aloud or in your mind, "Parking angel of Sun Yellow, Grass Green, and Sky Blue, I would like to request your help in getting me a parking spot [*specify where and when*]. Thank you in advance for your help."

4. When you receive that which you have asked for, thank the angel again. Angels work for gratitude and appreciation!

   In addition to stating your request clearly, the most important aspect of working with angels is that you thank the angel both ***in advance*** and ***after your request has been fulfilled***. If you learn nothing else about angels, learn this: it is very important to thank angels so they will be willing to help you later.

Angels have so many more resources than humans, and it can be a lot of fun to see how they go about solving our problems (not just finding parking spaces) and making our lives easier. For instance, help may come in the form of a person who shows up offering to do just what we need done. It may be in the form of new ideas that suddenly come to us on how to re-prioritize a busy schedule. It could be in the form of discovering a new tea or herbal substance that relaxes one before going to bed.

Finally, it may be that we won't know the form, only the results that caused one person to leave the parking spot in front of the doctor's office just as we pulled in, or why our surly boss was suddenly open and truly able to listen to our explanations.

Your job is simply to stay out of the angel's way once you have completed the ritual. Don't get caught up in details of how to make this happen. That is the angel's job. After all, if you could complete the request by yourself then you would not need to hire an angel.

Be careful to avoid setting too many parameters on your request. Give the angel room to have fun and be creative with their assignment and to use their judgment on the best way to accomplish your request. They can see a larger picture and know the best way to serve you without inconveniencing others.

HOW TO HIRE ANGELS FOR OTHER PURPOSES

Once you have used the ritual to hire parking angels for a few days, feel free to expand your requests to include other types of angels. The method is the same. Only the words of the request change. As always, be sure to express your appreciation both immediately after making your request, and after the angel has completed your request!

1. Say out loud or in your mind, "I would like to request a ________ angel of Sun Yellow, Grass Green, and Sky Blue." (These same spiritual colors are applicable to all angels.)

2. Wait until you feel the angel's presence, or just wait about 10 seconds.

3. Say aloud or in your mind, "________ angel of Sun Yellow, Grass Green, and Sky Blue, I would like to request your help with ________ [*be sure to specify the details of where and when of your request*]. Thank you in advance for your help."

4. When the angel has completed the task, remember to thank the angel again.

WHAT IF YOUR ANGEL DOES NOT DELIVER?

Angels very rarely fail to fulfill a request, however there are certain circumstances under which your request is either not fulfilled or *appears* not to be fulfilled. These circumstances might include the following:

- you have made an earlier request that is contradictory to this one... in this case, the angels usually give priority to the earlier request
- your request is contradictory to a larger aim or goal you have set for yourself, such as a yearly aim (for instance, if you have done a ritual to help you avoid chocolate, and then you ask an angel to help you find a chocolate shop, you can see how the angel might have some difficulty completing your request)
- your request has been fulfilled but in a way that you do not recognize
- your request would do harm to yourself or others, whether you realize it or not (angels want very much to evolve, and doing harm prevents them from their evolution... thus they are quite reluctant to fulfill requests that they know will do harm)

These are just a few of the circumstances in which an angel does not fulfill your request or appears not to fulfill your request. In either case, your best step would be to ask your angel for clarification. Ask the angel to show you or tell you ***in a way that you can easily understand*** the reason that it appears your request has not been fulfilled.

You will find that angels are more than happy to explain—and keep explaining—until you understand the situation. If you ask your angel for clarification and still do not understand why your angel appears to have failed in delivering on your request, keep asking. Your angel doesn't mind at all. In addition, the ongoing dialog will help you build a stronger and more lasting relationship with your angel or angels. Persistence and gratitude are both important factors to remember when working with angels!

9.3

BEGINNER RITUALS AND SPELLS

TALKING TO THE SPIRIT OF OWL TO FIND HIDDEN INFORMATION

If you need some information that you can't find on Google, such as some spiritual insight, you might check in with the Spirit of Owl.

The Owl totem has all of the best qualities of physical owls:

- extremely keen sight, especially at night (allowing them to see the hidden)
- excellent hearing
- the ability to turn their heads 270 degrees (giving them "eyes in the back of their heads")

- excellent hunting skills
- a reputation for wisdom

In short, if you need someone to "hunt down" some information for you, especially if that information is hidden, turn to the Owl totem.

The totem animal of Owl sees and knows the truth. Owl has wisdom and can see through the darkness. The Owl totem is a good one to work with if you want answers from the Universe. Owl medicine is associated with clairvoyance, astral projection, witchcraft, and magic. Owl sits in the East, which is the place of illumination and can see things that others cannot. While some tribes fear the Owl totem, considering it to be a pre-cursor to death, our experience with Owl has always been positive.

HOW TO REQUEST HELP FROM OWL

Working with the Owl totem is very similar to working with angels. Unlike angels, who are available for almost any life need, the Owl totem specializes in hunting down information that is hidden or not immediately available. To work with Owl, follow the steps of this ritual:

1. Say aloud or in your mind, "Spirit of Owl, I request your help."

2. Wait a few moments until you feel the presence of Owl (no more than a few seconds). Proceed to the next step if you are not sure if you "feel" Owl, since Owl always comes without fail.

3. State your request. For instance, if you need help understanding why you have suddenly become accident-prone, you might say, "Owl, please come with me today and show me what is causing these accidents in my life. Please show me in a way that I can clearly understand. Thank you in advance for your help." As with angels, the Owl totem thrives on appreciation so remember to thank Owl as soon as you have completed your request.

4. Keep an open mind to what Owl will show you. Owl will ride with you on your shoulder, whispering in your ear, giving you knowing and understanding where before you had only blindness and confusion. Owl may bring up old memories, send you a phrase from the mouth of a stranger or bring a chance meeting with another person. Owl will use any and every device to help you see. It could in the form of a conversation you overhear, finding a significant symbol or talisman, an owl that flies very near you at an opportune moment, or a magazine that falls open to an article with the very information you seek.

5. Once the Owl totem has shown you what you need to know, offer your appreciation and gratitude again. Totems, angels, and higher beings are not vain, but they certainly thrive on appreciation. You can never offer "too much" appreciation to these types of beings.

If at the end of the stated period of time, a day in the above example, you still don't understand what Owl is showing you, ask again the next day. When working with Owl, you are working with hidden information. Therefore, one possible outcome is that you don't understand the information that Owl sends you. Alternately, Owl sends you the information but it is still "hidden" enough that you missed it.

In either case, ask again. This time ask specifically for information in a form that you will be sure to understand. It could be that the way you phrased the question is the problem. Maybe you need to change the question to find out why you can't seem to "see" what you need to see. Like all rituals of magic or witchcraft, think through your question before continuing, and then make adjustments according to the responses you receive. Owl is very good at delivering the answers we need, we just have to ask the right questions.

As you keep asking, each day Owl will make it more obvious to you. The more you contact Owl in your daily magic practice, the faster these insights will come. Each time you gain a new insight or understanding, thank Owl for the help. Remember that Owl penetrates secrets and veils, and can show you anything you wish to know. All you have to do is be persistent in asking until you reach understanding.

9.4

Beginner Rituals and Spells

Bathtub Litany for Relief from Negativity and Pain

When you feel stressed, overwhelmed, or just plain fried, there's no magic like bathtub magic. This little ritual is soothing, fun, relaxing, pampering, and just plain wonderful. The bathtub litany is a great little ritual for the beginner practitioner of magic and witchcraft.

As an added benefit, this is one of the most healing rituals around, whether you are a beginner or an experienced practitioner. This ritual is effective for soothing all levels of pain, including physical inflammation and soreness, emotional frustration and anger, and repetitive mental thoughts that won't stop.

All of these health issues are expressions of excess Fire energy. Luckily, the bathtub litany ritual will take care of all of these. You can also do this ritual in the shower if you don't have time to actually soak in the tub!

HOW TO DO THE BATHTUB OR SHOWER LITANY

From a magical point of view, this ritual works because the element Water carries Fire energy. At the end of your bath, as the water drains out of the tub and you say the litany aloud in a voice of command, the element Water pulls any excess Fire energy from your body, mind, and Spirit. As the water flows down the drain, so does the excess Fire energy. For this ritual to work, you combine your intention with some visualization and the magic litany. While many people use a clumsy form of this technique intuitively, its effectiveness increases when done intentionally and precisely.

BATHTUB INSTRUCTIONS

Fill the tub as full as possible with cool (just below body temperature) water, but not cold water. Alternately, if you want to have a relaxing hot bath first, do so. Then follow the directions for this ritual as the water cools. If the water is too cold it will create tension, and if the water is too hot it won't carry much Fire energy.

Lie back with your feet at the drain end and as much of your body as possible under the water. As you lie in the tub, picture your body as a glowing heating coil. This visualization will push Fire energy into the water, warming the water next to your skin. As you do so, the Fire energy will follow natural body flows.

Stir the water each time this visualization seems to warm the water next to your skin. After three or four "stirrings," open the tub drain and continue to lay back and radiate the Fire energies as the water level drops around you. Say this litany out loud in a voice of command as the water drains from the tub:

All the tension, all the strain,

All the pain with excess flame,

Flow with water, down the drain!

Here's an alternate form that you can also use:

All the stress, all the strain

All the tension, all the pain

Flow with water, down the drain.

As the water flows down the drain, picture the Fire energies mixing with the water. Keep repeating the litany aloud.

Bathtub Litany for Relief from Negativity and Pain

Speak the litany with authority and power. Keep saying it until you feel that the excess Fire energy is gone. Continue the process until all the water is gone from the tub. At this point, you should feel more peaceful, relaxed, and physically at ease.

Use the litanies as given, experimenting with each for several weeks. After noticing and recording the differences, choose the one that best suits your personality and needs. Alternately you can switch between the litanies as needed. Some people write these litanies, put them in waterproof baggies, and tape them to the shower wall as reference sheets!

Shower Instructions

If you do not take baths or you tend to take more showers, you can use the same ritual in the shower. Set the water temperature so that it is cool but not cold (just below body temperature). Adjust the showerhead so the water hits you at the base of the skull and the water runs as evenly as possible over the back and front of your body. It is important to ensure that the water runs down the back of the neck because this is where many people tend to develop a lot of tension (in the shoulders).

As the water flows, run your hands down your body to bring the excess Fire energy down to your feet. Use the same glowing heating coil visualization as with the bathtub ritual. See the excess Fire energies being soaked up by the water, and flowing with the water down the drain.

At the same time, choose one of the litanies given previously and say it aloud with power and authority. Keep repeating the litany until you feel a change in your state. You may feel less physical pain, a lessening of anxiety, or a sense of peace in your mind. If you have a lot of mind chatter and you suddenly notice that your mind is quiet, then you know that the ritual has been effective. At this point, you may stop saying the litany and consider the ritual a success!

THE BATHTUB AND SHOWER LITANY AS SLEEP AIDS

Because this simple little ritual helps you get rid of excess Fire energies, it can help you sleep at night, especially if you regularly have trouble sleeping. This ritual works very well if you suffer from sleep problems because of:

- mind chatter
- anxiety
- physical soreness or pain or restlessness
- emotional issues that are weighing you down
- over-tiredness from mental overwhelm
- child-like excitement about current projects
- any issues related to power, will, pain, or excess/ repetition

To improve the power of this ritual, as you say the litany focus your intention and visualization on the specific issues that are bothering you. You can also try adding some lavender essential oils to your tub water for some extra aromatherapy soothing. Using this litany before going to bed can help release stress and tension, and get you relaxed and ready for sleep.

9.5

Beginner Rituals and Spells

Walking in the Rain by Running Water for Fresh Insight

If some of your old patterns and habits are getting in the way of you spiritual growth or enjoyment of life, it's time to let go of them. Sounds good, right? Unfortunately, letting go of old habits is often easier said than done.

Letting go of old beliefs and accepting new ones can be challenging no matter how long you've observed and worked on your inner life. Sometimes, we need a little help to pry loose the death grip we've got on our old ideas.

Walking in the Rain by Running Water for Fresh Insight

In tribal times people used the element Water as a source of cleansing and a way to help release the old and bring in the new. They would walk in the rain by running water. The running water carries away old ideas and beliefs that no longer serve. The rain, coming from above, brings clear, fresh, and new ideas to work with.

This ritual is also effective whenever you need to release any kind of negative emotion, stop repetitive negative thoughts, or rid yourself of low emotional tones like depression.

How to Do This Ritual

This ritual is very simple. In addition, this ritual gets you out into Nature, which will help you feel better regardless. To perform this simple ritual, follow these steps:

1. If you can, find a place in Nature where you can walk in the rain by running water (you would, of course, have to perform this ritual on a rainy day). If the weather is not rainy or you are living in drought conditions, you can use the shower ritual described earlier in this book. The shower also provides fresh water from above and running water below.

2. As you walk by or stand in the running water feel your old beliefs and worries fall away, being carried by the flow of the water to be recycled in some other form, in some other place in the Universe. Also release any repetitive thoughts, feelings of anxiety, and anything negative you want to release.
3. As you stand under the rain, feel the brightness and refreshment of the new bursting into your world—new ideas, new will to work, new expressions of creativity, and new feelings of all kinds.

If you want, you can also pray to whatever powers and beings inspire you, telling them exactly what you want to release and what you'd like to welcome into your life. Talk to powers and beings just as you would a good friend—you don't need to use any special language or formalities. Powers and beings are always listening to us. Choose the powers and beings with which you have the best affinity and relationship.

While this ritual may soak you through to the skin, which can sometimes be inconvenient, the effects are definitely worth the effort. It isn't often that we take the time to refresh ourselves in the course of our busy lives. Take a few minutes with this ritual and you'll find joy for many seasons to come!

Why This Ritual is Effective

In magic and witchcraft, the element Water represents emotions, which are the language of Spirit. In addition, moving water has the ability to carry the elements Air and Fire. The element Air magically represents thoughts, while Fire represents will and action. You'll notice that this ritual is based on the same spiritual principles as the bathtub and shower litanies.

By walking in the rain by running water while consciously "letting go" of negative thoughts, tension in the body, and negative emotions, you are performing a ritual that helps you rid yourself of unwanted negative energies.

One magical caveat here is that for this ritual to work, you need to have running water, not standing water. Unless specifically programmed, standing water is stagnant, and therefore does not do a great job of carrying negativity away from you. Standing water that has not been programmed ("charged") can receive negative energy from you, but it requires a lot of effort on your part to push that energy into the water.

A STORY ABOUT WALKING IN THE RAIN BY RUNNING WATER

Once upon a time, when I felt quite depressed and "stuck" in my life, a wise and magical practitioner told me to walk in the rain by running water. She told me that the running water would carry away my depression and negative emotions. The rain would bring fresh emotions and insight to me.

Thus, one rainy day I did walk in the rain by a fast-running creek. The combination worked and I felt immediately better. In fact, I emerged from this experience thoroughly soaked, as well as refreshed and positive.

I recently got to try that experience again, in Zion National Park, where we just spent two weeks playing in the wonders of Nature. Twice we hiked the Narrows, a hike that took us up the Virgin River through towering canyon walls. The water was clear, fast, and purifying. We hiked three miles up stream, then came three miles back down stream. When I emerged from the Narrows, I felt spiritually refreshed, as if I had just done a walking meditation. I wasn't feeling particularly negative before I hiked the Narrows, but even so I felt the magic capability of running water to refresh and rejuvenate.

— *Raven Wind Star*
California

9.6

BEGINNER RITUALS AND SPELLS

USING THE WATER BOWL FOR SCRYING AND PSYCHIC MESSAGES

The water bowl is a versatile tool of witchcraft that can be used for a variety of purposes, including scrying and sending psychic messages. Scrying is the art of looking for information that is not easily available in the ordinary world. In the practice of witchcraft, Water is the energy of Spirit, and flowing Water with a water bowl can help Spirit find desired information, or communicate with another Spirit.

WHAT IS A WATER BOWL?

A water bowl is simply a "bowl" formed by holding your elbows snug against your sides. You lace your fingers together in front of you to form a bowl, and visualize flowing your energetic Water into this bowl. This procedure takes very little time and handles a lot of life's daily difficulties. It also allows you to accomplish a lot without changing your overall water level, but simply re-circulating it. To make the most of your water bowls, read the following safety cautions until you understand them thoroughly:

- Flow only Water Blue (a bright blue) energy for this exercise. Do not flow dark blue, blue-black, or black.
- Be sure the "bowl" is at or above the level of your navel.
- Do not drop the bowl without first reabsorbing the Water energies in it (we'll show you how in the next section). If you accidentally drop the water bowl before you have reabsorbed all the Water, it may leave you short of Water which could produce a feeling of being emotionally drained or could cause dehydration. It could also possibly cause diarrhea. Also, keep the bowl level to prevent sloshing.

HOW TO BUILD A WATER BOWL

Building a water bowl is a simple procedure. With practice, it will take you only a minute or two to build one. In this section, we give you instructions on how to build a simple water bowl with smooth and calm Water. Once you have learned this procedure, we will teach you how to use a water bowl for other purposes, such as scrying. To build a water bowl:

1. Have a Water Blue color source (something bright blue) available as a reference.

5. Seat yourself so you can rest your elbows comfortably against your sides at or just above your hip bone points with your arms and hands extended horizontally or slightly up angled in front of you and the tips of your fingers interlaced. This results in a "bowl" at about the level of or just above your navel.

   High or low bowls will have different effects. Standing, you will only affect the area above and at the level of the arms. If you do a bowl too low or are bent over, it will affect intestinal tract, kidneys, or bladder. If you make one below the waist, it will trigger the body's mechanism for clearing Water and you will go to the bathroom a lot.

2. Envision or "mock-up" a dry stream bed or ditch descending from the region of your heart into the bowl on the side nearest you. Build a spout right above the heart and allow a stream of Water to flow down the ditch or stream bed into the left side of the bowl. Just see it in your mind's eye. You can also allow the Water to flow out of the spout directly into the left edge of the bowl. Be sure and look at your Water Blue source as you are flowing Water.

3. You can decorate the bowl on the edges if you so desire with palm trees, birds and flowers. The Water flowing down can be a cascading mountain stream or a fountain-like stream pouring into the corner.

   Fill the bowl, which should be a fairly deep bowl, until the Water reaches the edge. As the bowl fills, you will likely have a sense of a rising coolness or pressure in your linked fingertips. Begin reabsorbing the Water by pulling the Water in your hands and up your arms from the bowl's far side. You don't need to think about this—your body knows what to do. The goal with reabsorbing the Water—and re-circulating it in later steps—is to develop a smooth surface to on your water bowl.

4. As you absorb the Water energies, re-circulate the Water back out to the spout so you have a continuous flow.

5. If you have alligators in your water bowl and they are dark, leave them alone. If they are healthy and

you don't want them, you can blow them over the edge of the bowl.

6. As you re-circulate your Water, let the turbulent feelings rush out and down the stream bed into the bowl, as with a turbulent stream down a hillside, without concerning yourself about their source. The only goal here is to smooth out the feelings so you can function in your situation at this time. To accomplish this goal, you want to have a clear top surface so continue circulating the Water until it smoothes out.

7. Continue recycling until one of the following occurs:

   ➢ The outflowing Water is running smoothly in the streambed (usually takes three to five minutes).

   ➢ The outflow stops of its own accord, often with a "chug" feeling. Do not force a restart if this happens! A forced restart may trigger release of an overwhelming amount of suppressed or repressed fear, anger, and grief.

   ➢ When you stop flowing, either intentionally—having achieved a smooth surface in your water bowl—or because the Water stopped flowing spontaneously, pull all the Water back up into your palms and up your arms. Failing to pull all your Water energies back in may cause you to feel emotionally drained or physically dehydrated.

8. Unlace your hands. You have just completed a water bowl!

You can use the water bowl, as outlined in this procedure, consistently to clear out emotional "junk." If you do so, you will find that your moods will stabilize and you will experience a more peaceful state of being in your daily life. You can also release all forms of stress and tension accumulated during the day, and this technique works especially well if you tend to have trouble sleeping.

WHAT IS SCRYING?

Scrying is a form of divination, and can easily be done using the water bowl. Divination is a general term that means "to obtain, by psychic or spiritual means, information not readily available to the physical senses of the body." The water bowl allows messages coming in through Spirit's senses to be translated into physical information that your eyes and mind will allow. Divination tools like water bowls, Tarot cards and pendulums provide a conscious or physical-level channel for receiving the information.

Using a water bowl as a scrying tool can help you find lost or stolen objects or people, discover what is happening in distant locations, remember "forgotten" past lives and events, as well as explore future possibilities. Scrying can also be used to find other similar kinds of information, such as sources of personal internal difficulties. Be careful with some of these uses as you may experience powerful and unexpected emotional reactions within and from yourself.

In exploring the future with any form of scrying (or interpretation of dreams and visions for that matter) you need to thoroughly understand that:

- The future is not set or pre-destined. It may be changed at any time before it actually happens.
- Scrying, visions, and dreams of any particular future event are only probabilities based on an assumption that the "flows of change" currently operating will continue unchanged!
- If a divined, dreamed, or envisioned future event is not what you want to happen, do some research in the water bowl to discover the pre-event causes and change them! If you do that, the divined, envisioned, or dreamed event either will not occur at all or will occur differently than seen.

HOW TO SCRY WITH THE WATER BOWL

Scrying with the water bowl is a simple ritual. You simply build a water bowl, then use the bowl as a tool to find the information you seek. Follow these procedures to perform this ritual:

1. Construct your water bowl and do any self-balancing necessary until you have a smooth calm surface.

2. Generate an emotional feeling of curiosity and focus on questions such as:
   - For your past: "Where was I in..." or "What happened to me in…"
   - For your future: "What is likely to happen on my trip to…" or "What is likely to happen if I…"
3. Holding the focus, feeling and question, look into the water bowl (not through it) and wait for a picture or series of pictures to form. You may have to keep saying the question over and over until a picture forms down in the water bowl. A small percentage of people feel as if the image forms "psychically" behind their heads. If this happens to you, don't worry. This is perfectly normal. Just relax and focus on the image. As the picture starts to form, it won't cloud your water bowl, it will get clearer.
4. If you get a picture, but need more details or information, you can ask additional questions to clarify.
5. You can close your eyes and look at the Water with your "mind's eye" if you have trouble with your eyes open. You can also train your eyes to look into the water bowl by practicing looking at the space halfway between you and an object 20 feet away until you don't see the object, just the space.
6. In doing divinations for the future, if you are going to take a trip, you can ask for a mock-up of different

aspects of the trip. "What is likely to happen on my trip?" You can get a moving picture of going to the airport and getting on the plane.

If you run into something that does not look right or that is dangerous and threatening, you want to find out everything you can about that situation. Get a bigger view, such as the time of day, weather, the surroundings, and the events leading up to it. Then, on the trip, look for the pre-cursor signs to appear. If they appear, change something immediately (something completely different from your plan), and you will change the outcome. A small change in the present leads to a larger change in the future.

7. When you are done, reabsorb the Water.

Special note: With past and future divinations, be ready to handle unexpected and possibly intense emotions from yourself at any time.

FINDING LOST PEOPLE OR OBJECTS

You can use the water bowl to find lost or stolen objects, or lost people. When looking for a person who may or may not be alive (or anyone you haven't heard from in a long time), you may get "weird" pictures in the bowl (i.e. star fields, rainbow colors, or some kind of an infantile environment) if the person has "passed over" or if, at the time of your operation, is out-of-body.

Your field may also appear dark when you are looking for someone, this could indicate that they are probably not on the physical plane anymore. In these cases, we strongly recommend that you let them be—the person is not available either because they have reincarnated or are out-of-body.

When looking for lost objects, you may see a dark field if the object is in a dark location, such as a dresser drawer or a closet. Back up or zoom out until you see more details about the location, such as a dresser or closet. You can also zoom out or around and look for an address or city sign on a highway. Follow these steps to find lost people or objects:

1. Construct your water bowl as discussed earlier.
2. Focus on, "I wonder where __ is?" while generating an emotional feeling of curiosity. Use a mental picture of the object or person in your mind as the identifier.
3. Holding the focus, feeling, and identifier picture, look into the bowl and wait for some visual indicators to form in the bowl (a picture of the subject's immediate surroundings, or electric-white letters, words or numbers giving locational clues). You may need to keep asking "where" questions until you get concrete, specific details.
4. When you've gotten the information you're after, reabsorb the Water and disassemble the bowl.

SENDING PSYCHIC MESSAGES WITH A WATER BOWL

Since the magical element Water is directly related to the emotions, it makes a wonderful medium for sending psychic messages. One of the great aspects of using a water bowl for psychic communication is that you can actually hold Spirit-to-Spirit conversations with another person (if the recipient is willing). Because Water is associated with the emotions, conversations of this type will take place at an emotional and spiritual level.

Since Water can be compulsive, you want to be sure to keep your conversations relatively light and happy, the exception being when you are using water bowl communication for self defense (a topic too major to be discussed in this beginner's book). If you make your water bowl conversations too heavy and compel someone to certain detrimental behaviors without cause, the Universe will hold you responsible by Rules of the Road.

The compulsive quality of Water does, however, make the water bowl a useful means to recover stolen property or unpaid debts, or to banish someone who is harassing you. To use the water bowl for messages:

1. Make a water bowl and be sure that the surface is clear and calm. If it is not, use the techniques discussed previously (by flowing Water around your water bowl) to balance your energies until you get a clear, calm surface.

2. When the bowl is full, stop the inflow and hold the bowl quietly so the Water stays calm. Do not circulate the Water.

3. Get very interested in the person with whom you are communicating, and feel a strong desire to establish communication with them.

4. Put the person's face clearly in the bowl beneath the surface of the Water. This establishes a direct psycho-spiritual link. If you are having difficulty seeing the person's face in the water bowl you may shut your eyes.

5. Speak the message to the recipient as though she or he were actually present. Be sure to focus your attention on the message and recipient and nothing else.

6. Since the water bowl forms a two-way link, you are likely to receive a response from the person. The responses you receive may be very different from responses you would get in normal conversation because you are speaking directly to the person's Spirit, not the person's mind. The mind rationalizes and justifies while Spirit does not.

7. Repeat the message if you like. This will really get the message across to the person you are communicating with.

8. Once you have completed the message or conversation, disassemble the water bowl being sure to reabsorb all the Water energies.

9. When using a water bowl in these applications, if the Water becomes turbulent, cloudy, or steamy, or if you begin to get a headache or burning eyes, you are

pushing Fire into the bowl. Stop looking into the bowl for a moment, rebalance, relax. and restart, staying as level emotionally as possible.

You may want to repeat the water bowl communication for several days in a row, since repetition always improves the rate of reception.

9.7

Beginner Rituals and Spells

Walking Meditation for Those Who Can't Sit Still

Does a sitting meditation drive you crazy? If so, don't worry because you are not alone. Sitting meditation is not for everyone, especially very active people who have difficulty sitting still.

If you are one of the many people who just can't seem to get the hang of sitting quietly and turning off your mind chatter, we have a great meditation for you. We offer this walking meditation because meditation is such an important ritual in a spiritual practice. In addition, meditation has many well-documented health benefits. Thus we have a simple ritual that will help you meditate successfully… without ever having to sit still!

HOW TO DO THE WALKING MEDITATION

This simple, practical ritual is meditation in action. If you have a hard time sitting through a non-moving meditation, you might really enjoy this walking meditation. This meditation gives you a chance to tell the Universe what is on your mind, and to get some feedback. It is also a great way to connect with higher powers and beings. Here is how you perform this walking ritual:

1. Decide what amount of time or what distance you want to walk each day (you can adjust this later).

2. During first half of the walk you get to talk. Talk to your guides, your totems, your angels or the Universe in general. Talk about what's on your mind, what's going on in your life, or what you want or need. Talk about anything that's important to you or that you need help with.

3. During the return portion of the walk you get to listen. Take in everything your guides or the Universe is trying to express to you. Feel your feelings, feel the sensations in your body, hear the sounds around you, smell the smells, and take in the

sights. Be aware of any thoughts or feelings that come to you. Become an instrument of listening and absorbing.

Once you have completed this ritual, you may consider yourself a practitioner of meditation. If you take this walk at about the same time every day, you will have established a consistent connection with higher powers and beings. In other words, it's a scheduled appointment between you and your higher helpers. It is a time when you can truly connect, listen, and be heard.

Your life will increase in richness, depth, and understanding. This and the other rituals offered in this book will become like a maypole around which your life revolves with steadiness and strength.

THE BENEFITS OF MEDITATION

There are many benefits of having a mediation practice. On a spiritual level, meditation is used to create peace, joy, harmony, and manifestation in your life. Meditation is a way of creating sacred space, giving you a place to "get away" from the noise and rush of everyday life.

Meditation also allows you to be able to commune with Nature, listen to messages from higher powers, clear your mind, and open yourself to many other magical occurrences.

Creating a meditation practice for yourself is a way of inviting in your psychic skills.

On the physical level the benefits of meditation include lower blood pressure, a stronger immune system, and reduced stress. A regular meditation practice has been shown to increase serotonin levels in the body, which can help with the depression, headaches, and insomnia that are associated with low serotonin levels. All of these health benefits are even more true when the meditation is done while walking.

WHAT IF YOU FEEL LIKE THE MEDITATION ISN'T WORKING?

How often have you started a new program of change in your life only to feel discouraged three days later because "nothing is happening"? Or maybe you actually stick with a new ritual for a whole two weeks and you see some change, but the changes are not happening fast enough to suit your tastes.

What do you do? Before you decide that everything really is hopeless, take a moment to look at the process of change with the help of this magical principle:

> *"A small change in the present produces a larger change in the future."*

This is the basic principle we use in spell work. Translated into ordinary language, this principle means that if you make even the tiniest change today you will see bigger change in about a week. And that bigger change will lead to an even bigger change in about two weeks. And so on and so forth.

So let us suppose that you have started meditating as a part of your spiritual practice. Say you have decided to do the walking meditation for 15 minutes each morning. On the first morning of meditating you will probably notice an immediate change because the ritual is new and the changes are readily apparent. You're content that your new program of meditation is going to be useful and helpful. More importantly, a small and highly contagious molecule of change has been born.

NOW WHAT HAPPENS A WEEK AFTER YOU START MEDITATING?

Maybe you have had a really hectic week and you feel tired and irritable. All of sudden it seems like the 15 minutes of meditation is too much. That 15 minute walking meditation simply takes too much time, especially when so many other things are demanding your time. When you are in this state, you probably feel like nothing is happening, and that no change is occurring.

BUT "NOTHING IS HAPPENING" HARDLY DESCRIBES WHAT IS GOING ON INSIDE YOU.

That highly contagious molecule of change that was born the day you began meditating has been busy reaching out and touching and transforming other molecules inside you. Now a greater percentage of your molecules than ever before has the quality of quiet listening that you create during your meditation. The quieter you become inside, the more you are able to listen to your inner intuitive voice, the better your work will be, and the better your life will be. But the change is still too small for you to notice, especially compared to the roar of everyday life.

But meditation works like the equation of the penny doubling every day.

Have you heard of that equation? In this equation, you start out with a penny and you double the amount every single day for 31 days. While a penny might seem like a tiny amount (it is), the cumulative doubling effect of 31 days is fairly astronomical. Here is what you get at the end of each week:

Day 1: $0.01

Day 7: $0.64

Day 14: $81.92

Day 21: $10,485.76

Day 28: $1,342,177.28

Day 31: $10,737,418.24

So at the end of the month you have over $10 million. The same is true with your new meditation practice, but the key is how long it takes you notice the change.

If you stop and take the time to observe your life you will be amazed by how easily you are hypnotized by the incessant buzz and hum of daily activities. There's voice mail and email, gossip, your car running low on gas, the need to feed the cat, or all of your troubles at work. There are a million things that take up your attention while this small quiet molecule formed by your daily meditation goes around and changes you from the inside out.

THE DIFFICULTY LIES IN BEING AWARE OF CHANGE.

In the example with the penny doubling, it may take you 31 days—when you already have $10 million in your pocket—before you notice that something has shifted and life is different. But it's worth it, right? Ten million dollars is a lot of money.

So, as they say, don't give up on change five minutes before the miracle happens. Stick with your meditation practice, take the time to be aware of even the smallest positive changes in your life, and prepare to be awestruck in the near future at the giant transformations that have taken place!

9.8

Beginner Rituals and Spells

Walking Litany for Invisibility and Other Magical Effects

Like the Exit Ritual, the Walking Litany is one of the three forms of the Navajo Beauty Way. If you don't remember all the benefits of the Beauty Way ritual, we suggest you go back and re-read the section detailing all the magical effects of this ritual. In case you're wondering, the second form of the Beauty Way is called Day Greetings and Day Endings. We will not cover this form in this book, but it is just as magical as the other two forms.

Walking Litany for Invisibility and Other Magical Effects

The Walking Litany, unlike the other two forms of the Beauty Way ritual, is a walking spell that affects you, the magical practitioner. The Walking Litany puts up a temporary omnil (shield) around you, which can be used for invisibility or other magical effects.

What is an Omnil?

An omnil is a three-dimensional whirling protective shield. An omnil is a shield that stays with you wherever you go. The word omnil comes from "Ohm" and "Nil," which mean all and nothing. An omnil, which looks like an energy bubble, separates you from time, space and events, and can be programmed to deflect certain kinds of energies and experiences.

For example, you can program an omnil to deflect outside influences such as negative energy, gossip, contact with a certain person, or even the weather. You can also program an omnil to pull certain influences or thoughts out of your personal space, including the desire for sweets and negative thoughts.

When you program or "key" an omnil, it will deflect everything you program it to deflect and let in everything else. The beauty of an omnil is that the more times it deflects something the stronger it gets. If you don't program your omnil it will deflect everything, which is sometimes useful for meditation.

An omnil does not take you out of the local space, time, and event continuum in which you live. It simply separates you from certain events and influences that you specify. This differs from a full-cast circle, covered in later courses, that actually takes you out of all space and time. The symbol for both omnils and full cast circles is shown following:

Ø

You can use an omnil for everything from magical protection to invisibility.

HOW TO DO THE WALKING LITANY

There are many different forms of the Walking Litany (same as with the Exit Rituals). Each Walking Litany must be done for at least the circumference of two city blocks. Here is how you perform this ritual:

1. Before you begin, take note of your current condition. How do you feel physically, mentally, emotionally, and spiritually? This is important because the Walking Litany will generally change your state.

2. Walk for at least two city blocks (longer if you like) as you say this litany. Say the litany out loud in time with your footsteps, and use a strong voice of command.

3. Repeat the following litany in time with your footsteps for the entire walk:

   With power around me, I walk in the world.

   With power within me, I walk in the world.

   This one carries power.

   This one walks in power.

4. On completion of the litany, again take note of your state. What has changed? What is new and what is no longer there?

You have just completed a power walk using the Walking Litany. You can use the Walking Litany any time you feel a loss of personal power or to create a more positive state.

To use the Walking Litany to create a state of invisibility, simply change the verses as follows:

With invisibility around me, I walk in the world.

With invisibility within me, I walk in the world.

This one carries invisibility.

This one walks in invisibility.

LITANIES VERSUS CHANTS

Just so we are clear, here is a little clarification on the nature of litanies and chants. Many people confuse litanies with chants. They are not the same. A chant is any set of verbal commands or instructions to create a magical effect in the environment. A litany is a chant that is used to affect the operator or person saying the litany.

The Walking Litany in the Navajo Beauty Way and the shower litany are examples of litanies. The Walking Litany is used to create a stable datum or anchor points for the person saying it. The shower litany uses Water energy plus some Air energy to clear excess Fire. Both the Walking Litany and the shower litany affect the person saying them.

The verses used to charge the Firebowl and Chalice (outlined in Book Three of this series) are chants. With these verses you are affecting the environment around you, specifically your tools. Any time more than one person is doing a chant it is a chant, not a litany, because it affects more than one person—it is a group function. If more than one person did the Walking Litany at the same time it would become a chant.

So when you do the Walking Litany, you are in effect using a continuous spell that affects you. As you know, by Law of Attraction, when you are affected or changed, your life is affected or changed.

Another way of saying this is captured by this esoteric quote:

> ***"The level of your being attracts the level of your life."***

Walking Litany for Invisibility and Other Magical Effects

When you do the Walking Litany, you change your level of being, which means, by Universal law, that your life must change as well. If you want your life to change, the Walking Litany is the perfect magical avenue.

An Example of Using the Walking Litany to Set Intention

Recently we had some of the more advanced students in our school design their own magic rituals as part of their original research. One student came up with a fabulously fitting ritual, very in keeping not only with the here and now, but also with the effect that he wished to create.

The Very Cool Magical Ritual

So here was his situation: he had just moved into a new neighborhood and had had some less-than-positive encounters with his new neighbors. Wishing to restore harmony, both within himself and in his relations with his neighbors, he used an ordinary landscaping task to create a powerful ritual.

He needed to trim an olive tree that day. As he approached the tree, he realized that olive branches are the traditional symbols of extending peace to another party. Perfect. As he trimmed the olive tree, he used the Navajo Beauty Way Walking Litany to create a sacred space around himself, the tree, and the entire area surrounding the tree.

Then, to expand the circle of sacred space and restore

harmony, he carried an olive branch to each border of his property, saying the Walking Litany as he went. The Walking Litany is actually a spell in motion. By saying the Walking Litany as he carried and placed each of the olive branches, he was in effect putting up a magical spell matrix around his property and in contact with his neighbors.

He reported that he felt appreciative of his neighbor's efforts to beautify their yards after performing his self-created ritual to extend peace to his neighbors. Prior to the ritual, his emotions ranged between anger and scorn toward those neighbors, especially when the neighbor's yard improvement projects overlapped with his own.

The external results have yet to be fully played out, but without a doubt the ritual created an internal effect. Because an internal change in us always leads to an external change in the world, this student is bound to soon see the positive physical effects of his personal ritual.

9.9

BEGINNER RITUALS AND SPELLS

ROOTING YOURSELF IN MOTHER EARTH

With current life conditions, people are desperately looking for solutions in witchcraft and magic to solve immediate life problems. In the words of one person, "I need magic, and I need it now! My life is falling apart by the day. What do I do? Just tell me."

This person knew he needed some magical help but he had no magical knowledge... and not a lot of time to learn. Many people need magical help right now, which is great because it increases the amount of magic being practiced in the world, but can be scary for the people who need help right away!

So how does someone who knows very little about magic get the needed magical help right away?

Rooting.

THE MAGIC RITUAL OF GETTING GROUNDED

One of the best ways to weather the ups-and-downs of the current world change is to practice rituals that connect you with Mother Earth. These are rituals that ground you into the Earth, and they work because the Earth is huge and absorbs just about anything you throw at it.

Any magic ritual that grounds you, and connects you with the element Earth, will help you weather the storm. Now why is this? Because there are already a lot of Air, Fire, and Water energies zinging around, and these combined energies can often lead to fear, reactivity, negativity, and other junky emotions. Magically, these three elements represent the following:

AIR

Thinking, planning, and communication. In a highly-charged situation, this could lead to arguments, negative thoughts, or plans for revenge.

FIRE

Movement, action, desire, and will. If you are stressed, increasing your Fire energy by doing a Fire-based magic ritual could lead to road rage, frenetic but useless action, or a fist-fight.

WATER

Emotions, feelings, and the language of Spirit. If you already feel down about your situation, doing a magic ritual that is too Watery can make you feel even sadder, triggering negative emotions.

For all of these reasons, rooting rituals that ground you and connect you with Mother Earth are definitely useful during these topsy-turvy world changes!

HOW TO DO THE ROOTING RITUAL

Rooting is a great ritual for flowing Earth energies deep into the ground, releasing excess energies of any kind, pulling Earth energies into the body and mineralizing the body. To perform this ritual, follow these instructions:

1. Place your palms or heels on the ground. These are the parts of your body from which you will extend "roots."

2. Extend your roots out of your body, through the carpet or tile, into the sub floor and down into the Earth. Just imagine or "see" roots growing from your palms or heels and reaching into the Earth. If you are in a multi-level building, you will need to go through each level until you reach the Earth. If you are wearing shoes with thick soles, you may have to extend the roots out the sides of your shoes to avoid the soles.
3. Once your roots reach the Earth, keep extending them down through the topsoil and deeper layers until you reach bedrock. You will feel the bedrock as a more solid sensation than burrowing through the soil.
4. When you reach bedrock, dig your roots in, and lock them in.
5. With each exhalation, push excess tension, anger, frustration, sadness, distraction, or other unwanted energies through your roots into the bedrock. The Earth will easily accept these energies.
6. With each inhaled breath, pull up minerals and energies from the Earth for stability and balance.
7. Once you feel relaxed and nourished, pull your roots back up into your body. Just see the roots retracting and going back into your body. If you stand up without pulling in your roots, you will feel a slight "popping" sensation, and your body might be sore for a few days.

8. This is a very simple but highly useful magic ritual during times like these. If you are under a great deal of stress, do this ritual at least once per day to relieve daily tension and negativity.

Enjoy the relaxing sensations of connecting with Mother Earth. Don't worry about affecting the Earth negatively—she can handle any and all kinds of energies!

9.10

Beginner Rituals and Spells

Beginner Weather Working with Clouds

If you are interested in becoming a magical weather worker, then cloud magic is a great place to start. Magical weather workers can do truly incredible things, including altering the direction of storms, calling in moisture during droughts, and even influencing temperatures on a local or global level.

In terms of daily use, knowing how to work with weather can help you clear up an impending storm on the day of a big outdoor concert, alter the course of a snowstorm so you don't have to drive through icy roads, or bring in some local cloud cover so your plants don't wilt from the heat during a sizzling summer.

But before you can do all of these incredible things with weather, you'll need to start on a smaller scale. Start with cloud magic.

Cloud magic is simply the art of moving clouds around in the sky. You can reshape clouds, move them from left to right, or even drill a hole in an overcast sky to let some sunshine through.

HOW TO DO CLOUD MAGIC

Cloud magic teaches you to extend and use your energies, which you can later develop when working with the Winds of the four directions and larger weather systems. Follow these four steps to begin practicing cloud magic.

1. Choose to practice cloud magic on a day that has scattered, puffy clouds. Get into a comfortable position (either sitting or laying down) where you can easily see the clouds.

2. Choose a particular cloud to work with. Decide what you will do with your cloud. You can dissolve the cloud, split the cloud in half, shape it to look like an animal, extend one end of the cloud, or make the cloud taller. Whatever you choose, keep it simple. For instance, you may choose a cloud that already

looks like a duck, but a duck with a short tail. Choose to extend the duck's tail until it looks proportional to the rest of the body.

3. Shape the cloud using your thoughts and intention. See the cloud as you want it to be. Now superimpose that image over the actual cloud. You can also talk to the cloud or use your hands to shape the cloud. While you obviously can't touch the cloud with your hands, clouds are sensitive to force of movement in your hands as well as the energy your hands project.
4. Clouds are very reactive and easy to shape, but sometimes slow to move. If you work with your cloud for one to two minutes but very little seems to be happening, take a break for a few minutes, then look at your cloud again. You will probably see that the cloud has moved in the direction you pushed it. The cloud just took a while to get there.

As with all of these types of exercises, don't judge the result. Just keep practicing. Before long you will be delighted with what you can do with cloud magic. At that point you will be ready to move on to more complex weather-working techniques.

BONUS: FORECAST YOUR OWN WEATHER!

Once you have practiced cloud magic for a while, you may wish to try some more advanced weather-working rituals. For instance, you may wish to work with storm Spirits to bring rain into a drought-ridden area. Alternately, you may want to stop the rain so you can take your kids on a long-promised fishing trip.

Whatever you choose, the point is that, as a practitioner, you don't have to arrange your life around the weather. There are things you can do magically to work with the weather. There are many ways of working with weather, and different disciplines use different techniques. Here are a few preparatory basics and some techniques you can use without a lot of specialized training.

CHECK WITH YOUR HIGHER POWERS

Angels or totems or Sky and Earth beings from the Exit Ritual know about the weather. There may be plans in the works or reasons of which we are unaware for a particular type of weather. If you get such a message of "plans in the works," leave the weather alone lest you suffer the consequences from Rules of the Road.

ASK WEATHER BEINGS FOR HELP

There are many higher beings or Spirits that are helpful when weather working. Different disciplines and traditions have their favorites or call them by various names. We find the Winds of each direction, Sky Father, weather angels, storm Spirits, sylphs and of course Earth Mother (we call her Grandmother) appropriate beings to consult.

Asking these beings for help creates a safer way to achieve the results you desire, since these beings exist on a higher level than we do and have access to higher levels of information. They are privy to a larger scale picture concerning what we are asking and will know how to help us without interfering in a bigger plan or inconveniencing another.

BE SPECIFIC IN YOUR REQUEST

As with all magical procedures, you need to thoroughly think through what you want and how you ask. For example you might say, "I want rain." A common result is that there will be no rain in your area, but rain might have occurred in the next county. The reason is that your statement did not include any specifics on where and when you wanted the rain to appear. Nor did you specify how much rain you wanted in what period of time. As a practitioner, it is your responsibility to be as specific as you can in defining what you are asking for.

FOCUS YOUR INTENTION

Now that you have defined exactly what you desire and have the help you need, see a picture of this in your mind. Focus your intention on this ideal picture, and lay this picture over what you see outside.

Put enough energy into the picture that you feel it coming alive. Focus on what you do want, not on what you don't want. People love to talk and complain about the weather. Don't let yourself get sucked into this energy. The "as above, so below" principle defines that the weather conditions will match the conditions of the land and people below it. Feeding this negative energy will delay or negate your intention.

Keep Your Emotions in Check

Whereas you need some emotional energy to push into your picture, be careful of too much or the type of energy you are flowing. Feelings of anxiousness, being distraught, scared, over-excited, nervousness, or other strong emotions can flow energies that will negatively affect your results.

Look for Small Changes You Can Make

Take a look at the current weather outside from the perspective of what one thing could you change that would lead to other changes. It takes less energy and less work to create one small change. Also remember that a small change in the present can lead to a large change in the future.

For example, you might move those dark clouds over and send them in a direction away from you. This could cause other like clouds to follow it and allow the sunshine to come through. Now it is clear enough and dry enough to take that fishing trip. Or maybe there are clouds that you can darken and add moisture to so your lawn gets that needed rain.

Try experimenting with different weather conditions and record your techniques and results so you know which work best for you. Following the above safety tips, you can have fun seeing your results improve as you practice.

A CONVERSATION WITH A STORM SPIRIT

I am sitting here enjoying an absolutely lovely flash-bang thunderstorm, and remembering a long-ago conversation I had with a storm Spirit. Back in the early days of my studies in magic and witchcraft, I was given the assignment to go out and communicate with a Nature Spirit, be it a Spirit of tree, rock, or sky.

Being naturally of an excitable temperament myself (being a triple Fire sign, astrologically), I chose to communicate with a storm Spirit. I waited until a particularly heavy storm hit our area, and then went out to have my first person-to-storm chat. The results were startling.

The long and short of the conversation was that storm Spirits don't much like people, and with good reason. During my chat with the storm Spirit, I raised the issue that the Spirit seemed quite angry and aggressive. The storm Spirit replied that it was a bit angry, especially with people, because most people did not like storms and did not want them around.

I replied that this was not entirely illogical, since storms could be inconvenient, causing a lot of destruction and wet. The storm Spirit huffed about that, I can tell you! He said that storms were a necessary part of the ecosystem, and that people did not properly appreciate their role. Storms cleanse the air and the land, and distribute water where it is needed. He added that it took a lot of force to do all of this cleansing and moving of water. He, like most storm Spirits, was fast-moving and very direct. He didn't have a lot of time to chat.

The biggest reason he disliked people, he said, was because most people talked about him but not to him. He said many people were quite negative about storms, in general, and cursed them. Unlike the people of ancient tribes, who properly appreciated the role storm Spirits played in the ecosystem, modern people only see the inconvenience of storms.

The storm Spirit and I ended the conversation on good terms (he was in a hurry to move on). I discovered a new appreciation for storms and the Spirits who create them. I've since had several more conversations with storm Spirits, some of which were even in the process of forming tornados. In my experience, storm Spirits start out angry. They like to clobber the landscape and be aggressive, but once you get them talking they tend to lighten up. And you have to talk fast, because storm Spirits don't have a lot of patience for idle chatter. They are all about action.

If you want to deepen your connection with the world of Spirits, storm Spirits can be interesting conversational partners, when you can make yourself heard. If you do decide to try communicating with storm Spirits, be sure to hail them out loud and welcome them. Since these Spirits are used to be cursed rather than welcomed, don't be surprised if your first greeting is met with a salvo of wind and rain. Just hang in there and keep shouting out your greeting until the Spirit hears you. The conversation is sure to be a revelation!

— *Raven Wind Star*
California

9.11

BEGINNER RITUALS AND SPELLS

PROTECTION AND DISCONNECTION LITANY

People ask us all the time how to protect themselves magically using self defense magic. Magical self defense is not difficult, but the procedures could boomerang if you are not sure you are in the clear according to self defense laws.

Practitioners of magic and witchcraft, having considerable power and force, need to carefully study self defense laws. Using our powers inappropriately can cause severe Universal backlash. We must be sure that we keep our tempers in check and not use our abilities in a reactive manner.

Western magical practice states:

> ***"You have a right to be here and follow your own path so long as you hinder no one else in doing likewise."***

This principle asserts our right to exist and follow our own path and thus our right to defend ourselves against those who would seek to prevent us from walking our path.

As we increase our magical abilities, we will attract the attention of beings of different levels and some of these will try to interfere with our path in one way or another. Clarissa Estes, author of *Women Who Run with the Wolves*, states this as, "If you have beauty in your life, know that it will attract the dark as well as the light. Don't be surprised. Be prepared."

As practitioners, we follow this very specific statement when it comes to self defense:

> ***"In cases of direct and violent personal harm you are entitled to defend yourself by any means available provided you did nothing to encourage or provoke the attack."***

Here we define some of the terms in the self defense statement so that there is no confusion.

DIRECT

Means upon body, mind or Spirit. A direct threat in spiritual, magical and witchcraft definitions includes attempts by any outside force or influence to drain your energy or impose their will upon you.

VIOLENT

Means anything that is damaging to your physical, mental, emotional, or spiritual well being. It does not matter what the attacker's intentions are, only the results.

ENCOURAGE

Means creating or permitting unnecessary opportunities for a known hostile being to attack you.

PROVOKE

Means being overly pushy when you know someone has a particularly sensitive area or is under a lot of stress, whether it is internal or external.

BY ANY MEANS AVAILABLE

Means using any means that you choose to defend yourself when attacked. As long as all the other conditions of this rule are met the Universe does not judge whether your response is excessive.

In some spiritual systems, it is considered a crime not to defend yourself because in so doing you are enabling the attacker to not learn appropriate spiritual behavior and impeding their spiritual growth. Any infringement on your sacred space gives you the right to defend yourself according to magical self defense laws.

Self defense tactics can come in very useful in a variety of situations and even be life-saving. Just remember to think them through and make sure you are on the right side of the self defense laws. Do not overreact, keep your cool, and make sure you are within your magical rights to use whatever technique you are considering. This will keep you in alignment with the Universe and prevent any backlash.

A NOTE OF CAUTION FOR BEGINNERS

If you are a beginner practitioner, this is note of caution about using spells and rituals for self defense. As a beginning practitioner, it is not uncommon to go through a period of increased awareness and sensitivity. During this period it can be easy to misinterpret increased sensitivity as being under attack. It is best to err on the side of caution when choosing a technique to employ and use those that cause lesser harm until you are sure that you are meeting the conditions appropriate for the use of magical self defense.

HOW TO DO THE DISCONNECT RITUAL FOR PROTECTION

One of the best and simplest rituals for self defense for beginner practitioners is the disconnect ritual. This simple ritual cuts you off, on multiple levels, from someone who is attacking you or your sacred space. Follow these instructions to perform the ritual:

1. Choose the person from whom you wish to disconnect.
2. Focus on that person with all your intention, and use a voice of command, out loud, to say the following ancient disconnect litany to the person. It does not matter that the person is not anywhere near you—the disconnect litany will disconnect you from that person, regardless of where they may be.

    I am neither your creature nor your get,

    To be moved by your whim or your let;

    I will go my own way,

    By night or by day,

    To serve my own purposes yet.

3. If there is another person from whom you wish to disconnect, repeat the process. Keep repeating the process until you have disconnected from all desired people. Remember to only use this litany as a form of magical self defense!

IMPROVE THE PERFORMANCE OF YOUR SELF DEFENSE RITUALS

One of the most common requests that we receive is from people who want to perform "revenge spells" for self defense. Unfortunately (or fortunately) the term "revenge spell" is an oxymoron. Most people think of revenge when they feel they have been wronged... and are feeling very negative! That's why a magic spell won't work in this case... because ***negativity and magic are mutually exclusive.***

To understand why this is so, you need to understand why magic is so magical. Magic is really nothing more than the Operating Laws of the Universe working as they should. Unfortunately, most people operate under the Law of Accident, which is on a level lower than the Operating Laws of the Universe. Magic can't operate at the level of the Law of Accident—it's too low. When a person who normally lives at the Law of Accident becomes positive enough to raise their energy to the next level, what seems like magic happens! It's really just the Operating Laws of the Universe, but it appears to be magic.

All of this is a long-winded explanation of why revenge spells don't often work. Self defense spells, when done with a cool head and positive energy, do work. But if you wait until you feel downright negative before you start looking at magic, forget it. You have to be positive and upright (virtuous) in your self defense for magic to work.

PRACTICE MAKES YOU READY

Protection magic and self defense tactics don't just come naturally to most people. Just like using martial arts for self defense, the moves have to be practiced before they are actually needed in a self defense situation. Waiting until you are under attack to try out your magical self defense tactics can prove to be very ineffective.

So what's the moral of this story? Practice your disconnect litany and the other rituals in this book so that you will be ready to use them when you need them!

10

SIMPLE RITUALS AND SPELLS

RITUALS AND SPELLS DONE WITH HOUSEHOLD INGREDIENTS

10.1 Simple Rituals and Spells

Sun Candle Blessing Ritual

The Sun Candle Blessing ritual is a really simple one that will help you stay positive, and create forward progress in your life at any time. This ritual has many benefits, and there are so many ways you can use the Sun Candle Blessing, including:

- clearing your house of negative energies
- creating sacred space
- lifting your spirits
- lifting someone else's spirits
- giving yourself a much-needed energy boost
- acting as an aid to meditation

- giving you mental energy for studying or clear thinking
- preventing negative energies from settling into your sacred space
- increasing your sense of personal power
- giving people greater ability to make choices
- creating harmony in a group of discordant people
- offering healing energy to someone going through hard times
- attracting positive events and outcomes

The Sun Candle Blessing ritual is effective because it uses the Fire energy Sun Yellow, which is useful for overcoming negative states because this color promotes Spirit Fire, creativity, motivation, and radiance. The act of burning the candle actually "pushes" these energies toward you and out into the room. This makes the Sun Candle Blessing ritual the perfect magical act for so many situations!

What You Will Need for this Ritual

- a Sun Candle of pure yellow (a bright yellow candle that has no red or orange or tones)
- wooden or paper matches (no lighters)
- a compass to find the cardinal direction South (no guessing)

- pen and paper (either a journal or book of shadows dedicated to your practice)
- a table and chair, with the chair in the South facing North and the table in front of the chair

For beginning practitioners, we suggest using the glass-encased yellow candles that can be found in the religious aisle of most grocery stores. While some of these glass-enclosed candles have images of religious icons, most stores also carry plain yellow candles (you want the plain yellow ones). These candles are perfect for the Sun Candle Blessing ritual because the color is usually pure yellow, and the glass provides a measure of fire safety.

Some advanced practitioners tend to carve a tribal sun symbol on a pure yellow candle, but that is not necessary for this ritual to be effective—nor do we suggest you take the time to carve a candle at this point. The act of carving would only hinder your forward progress, and we want you to get the benefits of this great multi-purpose ritual as soon as possible!

For this ritual, you will use *only* paper or wooden matches. The reason is that most lighters have butane, which contains ingredients that can cause unwanted side effects if used in this ritual.

You will also need a compass to help you find the cardinal direction South. In our tribal traditions, most of our spells and rituals are performed with the practitioner sitting in the South, facing North. You may need to step outside to use your compass, as the electromagnetic energy in your house may interfere with your compass reading.

HOW TO DO THE SUN CANDLE BLESSING RITUAL

Awareness of change is an important part of the Sun Candle Blessing ritual. In other words, performing this ritual always has a positive effect, but beginner practitioners may not be sufficiently aware of those changes at first. Hence, they may not think that the ritual is effective. That's why the first step of this ritual is all about awareness. Follow these steps to perform the Sun Candle Blessing ritual:

1. Place all of your materials in front of you on your table. Sit in the South and face North.

2. Take a few moments to write how you feel in your journal or book of shadows. Take note of your physical, emotional, and mental states, as well as any "issues" that are bothering you or keep recurring as nagging thoughts. You will return to your journal or book of shadows at the end of this exercise.

3. Light the candle using wooden or paper matches (do *not* use a lighter).

4. Wait until the candle flame is steady and tall (this type of flame is called a "working flame," and most practitioners wait until they have a working flame before proceeding with any kind of candle magic).

5. Cup your hands around the flame, focusing your attention on the candle and flame.

6. Charge the Sun Candle by saying the following charge verse in a voice of command (a strong, powerful voice). Charging is the process of "programming" a magical tool, such as the Sun Candle, to perform a specific act.

   Child of Wonder,

   Child of Flame,

   Nourish My Spirit,

   And Protect My Aim!

   If there are other people in the room with you, change the word "My" to "Our." Also change the word "Spirit" to "Spirits."

7. Leave the candle burning in the room for at least 30 minutes (be sure the candle is on a protected surface such as a plate and is not a fire hazard).

8. At the end of 30 minutes, or when you feel ready, blow out the flame (don't snuff it).

9. Spend a moment or two in the area to see if you can detect a difference in the level and quality of energy in the area—in yourself. Both you and the area in which you did the ritual should feel lighter, more harmonious, and/or more peaceful. Write your impressions in your journal or book of shadows. Compare your descriptions from before and after you did the ritual.

We suggest that you perform this ritual for 30 minutes each day for 40 days. Each day be sure to journal about your experiences, feelings, and sensations before and after the ritual. You will be surprised at how effective this simple spell can be. For a beginner practitioner, the Sun Candle Blessing ritual is a perfect way to build a solid practice of witchcraft and magic.

How to "Clear" Multiple Rooms with the Sun Candle Blessing Ritual

In the previous set of directions, we gave you instructions on how to charge the Sun Candle to affect you and the area immediately around you. For instance, you will probably notice that the Sun Candle Blessing ritual affects your mood. At the same time, the ritual will probably positively transform the energy in the entire room.

But what do you do if you want to clear more than one room of negative energies? You can achieve this in two ways. You can either use multiple Sun Candles, or you can use a single Sun Candle and move it around your house.

If you want to clear all the rooms at once, you will need multiple Sun Candles. Place a Sun Candle in each room, the follow the directions given earlier to light and charge the candle in each room. Let each candle burn for 30 minutes or more before blowing it out.

If you want to clear your rooms one by one, you can light and charge the candle in one room and let it burn for 30 minutes. After 30 minutes carry the candle into the next room you want to clear, and charge it again without blowing it out. You can clear your entire house this way. Note that you must "recharge" the Sun Candle each time you move it to a new room.

If there is a room that feels like it has particularly negative energy, you may want to let the candle burn for more than 30 minutes. Sometimes letting the Sun Candle burn for one to two hours is necessary to clear the room. Use your judgment and "feel" to help you determine when the candle has done its work.

If the candle flame sputters or is dampened (burns very low) when you light it or after you charge it, then the room probably has enough negative energy that you will need to let the candle burn for longer than 30 minutes. In addition to using your own spiritual senses, you can check the height of the candle flame to determine when the Sun Candle has cleared the room. When a dampened flame transforms into a consistently tall and bright "working flame," the Sun Candle has completed the clearing.

HOW TO USE THE SUN CANDLE FOR PARTIES

Using the Sun Candle is a great idea if you want to have happy energy at a party. Before the party starts, go ahead and clear every room in your house with the Sun Candle Blessing ritual.

If you have invited people to your house who normally produce negative or unpleasant energy, then you may wish to keep one or more Sun Candles burning during the actual party. Burning the candle during the party will keep the area clear of negative energies and preserve your sacred space.

To most people the Sun Candle looks just like an ordinary candle, so burning it won't attract much attention. Burn the Sun Candle in every room affected by the party. The charged Sun Candle will act as a sort of shield, or ***psychic teflon***, and prevent junky energies from settling into your house.

In addition, people who are especially loud or obnoxious will be repelled by the candles (although they won't know why). These people will tend to find an excuse to leave the party early! Once the party is over, you may want to let the candles burn for another 15 to 20 minutes before blowing them out just to be sure all the negative energies have been cleared.

As you can probably tell, having a good supply of Sun Candles is useful. If you are going to use Sun Candles frequently, we suggest you buy the larger pillar candles or multiple yellow candles in glass (the type found in the religious aisles of most grocery stores).

With the large pillar candles, only the outside needs to be pure yellow, since the color on the outside of the candle determines its effect. The inside of the candle can be white. If you plan on burning these candles regularly, we suggest you burn each on a large plate as a fire safety precaution. With the candles that are encased in glass, be sure that there are no pictures or words on the glass, since this could inadvertently program the Sun Candle in unexpected ways!

When you burn these candles, we suggest you place them on large plates as well for fire safety.

HOW TO HELP SOMEONE ELSE WITH THE SUN CANDLE BLESSING RITUAL

Does someone in your life need a little boost, or even a big boost? You can charge and burn the Sun Candle for someone else, even if they don't live anywhere near you. Remember that the Sun Candle produces energy that nourishes the Spirit so this ritual is particularly good for people who feel depressed or low, or even for people who may be dying. Sun Yellow energy is the only energy that gives people greater ability to make choices.

To charge the candle for someone else, sit or stand in the South facing North with your candle in front of you as usual. After lighting the candle with a paper or wooden match, change the charge verse to reflect the name of the person you want to help. For instance, if you want to help a person named Amy Johnson, you would use this charge verse (while focusing your intent on Amy):

Child of Wonder,

Child of Flame,

Nourish Amy Johnson's Spirit,

And Protect Her Aim.

You can burn your candle for this person daily if that

would be useful. Location is not a barrier for energy, so even if the person is halfway across the world the Sun Yellow energy will get to them.

How to Boost Your Own Energies All Day Long

Do you have a day of arduous work or effort coming up? Are you packing up and moving your house, or meeting with people all day? If so, you can burn your Sun Candle all day to give you energy and spiritual support throughout.

Light and charge your candle as usual, then put it in a safe place where you can check on it regularly. For instance, if you are working at home you might want to put the candle on a plate and put both plate and candle in your kitchen sink, which is fireproof. Just make sure there is nothing flammable around the candle, and be sure to check on the candle every hour or so.

Many people who do bodywork, such as massage, Reiki, or energy healers, burn the Sun Candle all day to keep themselves clear of other people's energies. Some burn the candle right in the room where they are working to help both themselves and their clients.

The Sun Candle can seem small and insignificant compared to all the big things we have to attend to each day, but never underestimate the power of Sun Yellow. When you study magic at a deeper level you will see that energy drives the world, not physical action. More importantly, the quality of energy that you project into the world determines the types of events and people you will encounter. The more you are filled with Sun Yellow, the more you will attract uplifting and bright events and people!

THE SUN CANDLE BLESSING RITUAL AS A FIRE MAGIC SPELL

Everything in this Universe is made up of some combination of the four magical elements: Air, Fire, Water, and Earth. The Fire element is associated with will, personal power, and creativity. Fire is also the action-oriented and motivational part of any creation and manifestation.

Magically speaking, once you have developed the idea of what you want to create (and done the planning part) in the Air element, it is time to move into Fire, where you take action and endeavor to bring your creation into being.

Fire is associated with the direction South, which is also the direction in which we perform all major spell work and creation. Specifically, Fire corresponds to:

> *...energy, power, will, desire, anger, pain, motivation, radiance, passion, initiative, aggression, limitation, endeavor, activity,*

> ***creativity, willingness, urge, inspiration, excitability, courage, bravado, compulsion, fanaticism, frustration, resentment, rage, freedom...***

If you want to affect any of these areas in your life, then you need to work with Fire. Unlike Air, which has only three colors, Fire has six major colors:

Sun Yellow: Spirit fire, creativity, radiance

Yellow-Orange: motivation, excitability, activity

Red-Orange: anger, pain, fever, aggression, drive

Bright-Red: courage, bravado, will, endeavor

Deep Red: passion, flow

Electric-Blue: all bands, initiating force on galactic or universal levels

As you can see, Sun Yellow is an excellent and safe color for the beginner practitioner to use for healing, cleansing, and gaining an energy boost. Sun Yellow has none of the potential of the Fire colors to create unwanted side effects, such as anger, nervousness, or excitability. For beginner practitioners, Sun Yellow is the perfect way to start playing with Fire energy. Stay away from the other Fire colors until you have much more experience with Fire energy, lest you do harm to yourself and others!

10.2

Simple Rituals and Spells

Relocating Unwanted Spirits Away from Your Home

Do you keep losing your keys and other small objects? Do you hear cabinet doors slamming in the middle of the night? Is something causing your dogs to bark at nothing at all?

If so, then you may have one or more unwanted Spirits in your home. This is not unusual, nor anything that you need to particularly fear. Many times Spirits who have not "moved on" hang around a house, either because they are familiar with the house, or simply because they like something about the house.

Relocating Unwanted Spirits Away from Your Home

Sometimes these Spirits are not aware that they no longer have physical bodies, and simply "carry on" with life as usual, even though they are now purely Spirit energy.

For instance, when we moved into an old farm house, we would often see a Spirit sitting in an old barrel chair in our living room, particularly during our morning meditations. When we described this Spirit, a very thin old man wearing jeans and a red checkered shirt, to one of our neighbors, we discovered that he used to live in our house. He simply "hung around" during meditations, liking the feel of the barrel chair. Eventually, though, he made us a little uncomfortable so we gave the very old chair to the pastor of a church. The Spirit of the old man left with the chair, and never returned.

What to Do if You Have a Spirit in Your Home

What should you do if you have an unwanted Spirit in your home? There are multiple options, none of which are difficult or scary. You might try one of the three following options.

1. Learn to Live with the Spirit

Our neighbors also live in a very old farm house that is inhabited by a Spirit who is mischievous rather than dangerous or harmful. He likes to slam kitchen cabinet doors at night, when the house is dark and quiet.

What do our neighbors do? Nothing too drastic. When they hear him banging the doors, they just yell "Stop that!" or "Cut it out!" Oddly enough, that is all it takes to keep him quiet. Since he does not get into any other kind of trouble, they leave him be the rest of the time. Most Spirits do not like to be yelled at and are afraid of loud noises, so this often works when a Spirit is up to naughty tricks.

2. TALK TO THE SPIRIT

Many Spirits have no idea that they no longer have bodies and are "hanging around" where they are unwanted. If you can see, sense, or feel the Spirit, then you can talk to him or her. You hold a conversation with a Spirit mostly as you would with another person.

There are two main differences between conversing with Spirits and chatting with your friends. First, some Spirits are quite "down tone" and may not respond to you right away. Don't worry. This is perfectly normal. Talking to a "down tone" Spirit is sort of like speaking to a depressed person—you may not get much of a response at first. Just keep asking questions and talking to the Spirit until you get a response.

The second difference between talking to a friend and speaking with a Spirit is that the Spirit's "answers" may sound like a voice in your head rather than an actual voice. This is normal since the Spirit does not have a body, so cannot speak out loud.

Once you engage the Spirit in conversation, start asking questions about the last lifetime in which the Spirit had a body. Ask for the Spirit's name, the time period in which he or she lived, and any other relevant details.

Finally, bring the conversation around to the happiest time the Spirit can remember in that lifetime. This memory of a happy time should bring the Spirit up in emotional tone, and allow him or her to move on. You may want to help the Spirit by asking him or her to move on, or offer to help him or her find a new body (in a tree, cloud, or rock, for instance). Once you make the suggestion—and the Spirit chooses a new body—he or she will mostly likely move immediately out of your house into his or her chosen rock, tree, or cloud.

3. Do a Two Element Cleansing Ritual

This option is a last resort, and should only be used if the Spirit in your home is really bothersome—or refuses to speak with you and move on. While these kinds of Spirits do exist, most Spirits are relatively harmless.

One way to discover whether a darker Spirit inhabits your space is to cut a clove of garlic in four equal sections. Place one section of garlic in each cardinal direction in your home. If one or more of the hearts of the garlic cloves turn dark within 24 hours, then you do indeed have a darker Spirit cohabitating with you. At this point, a two-element cleansing ritual (of the magical elements Air and Fire) is called for.

WHAT YOU WILL NEED FOR THE TWO ELEMENT CLEANSING RITUAL

- a Sun Yellow candle
- a smudge stick made of cedar and sage
- wooden or paper matches (no lighters)
- a compass to find the cardinal direction South
- pen and paper (either a journal or book of shadows dedicated to rituals)

HOW TO DO A TWO ELEMENT CLEANSING RITUAL

This ritual uses the magical elements of Air and Fire (as represented by the cedar and sage in the smudge stick) to move noxious Spirits out of your home. Most bothersome Spirits dislike the magical energies of cedar and sage, and would rather get away from the smoke created by burning these plants. To do a two element cleansing ritual, follow these steps:

1. As usual for most types of rituals and spells, seat yourself comfortably in the South while facing North. Place all the items you will need for this ritual on a table in front of you.
2. Using paper or wooden matches, light and charge the Sun Candle as described previously. Wait until

the Sun Candle has a tall working flame before proceeding.

3. Light the smudge stick by holding it in the flame of the Sun Candle. Once the stick is lit, blow Sun Yellow energy gently on it until it is producing a thick dense column of smoke. To blow Sun Yellow energy onto the smudge stick, simply look at Sun Candle as a color reference, and see that yellow energy being blown onto the smudge stick. The element Air carries Fire energy, so you breath will easily carry Sun Yellow energy.

4. Charge or program the smudge stick, much as you did with the Sun Candle Blessing ritual. To charge the smudge stick, say the following verse in a voice of command, blowing Sun Yellow energy onto the smudge stick before and after the verse, as well as between each line of the verse:

Fire and Air where you are cast,

Let no spell nor adverse purpose last,

Not in accord with me!

Cleanse these walls and cleanse this space,

Far from here send baneful trace!

Thus my will, so it be!

If you later wish to use the smudge stick for other cleansing purposes, you may substitute or add verses to suit your purpose. For instance, here are some substitutions or additions you can make:

Add or Substitute	"Cleanse these tools and cleanse their space"	To clean magical tools and simulacra
Add or Substitute	"Cleanse these people and cleanse their space"	To cleanse people before a ritual or anytime
Substitute	Anger, grief, trauma or any other applicable term for "spell" or "adverse" or "baneful." For instance, substitute "fear" for spell. Substitute "cancer," "anger" or "sickness" for "adverse purpose" or "baneful."	To apply to specific circumstances so long as the rhythm of the verse is not disturbed.

5. Once you have charged the smudge stick, carry it with you and move to the center of the East-most wall of the area you want to cleanse (see the following figure of the room diagram). If you want to cleanse your entire house, go to the East-most interior wall of the East-most room in your house. If your house has multiple stories, start on the lowest story and work your way up. If you are cleansing just an area, go to the East-most wall of that area.

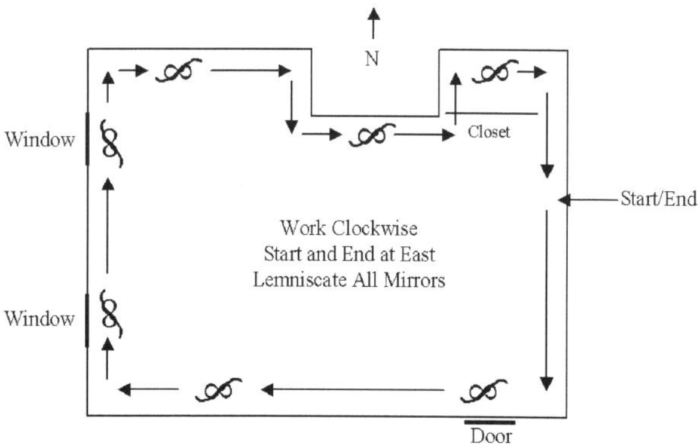

6. Facing the wall, move the smudge stick so that the smoke from the bowl creates a Lemniscate on the center of that wall about chest height. A Lemniscate looks like a "Lazy 8" or the infinity symbol (∞). See the Lemniscate figures in the previous room cleansing diagram. As you smudge the wall watch the smoke to make sure it "sticks" to the wall (i.e., doesn't bounce off the wall). If the smoke bounces off, draw another Lemniscate (or several more) until the smoke sticks.

7. Move clockwise or to the right down the wall, holding your smudge stick chest high, allowing the smoke to trail along the wall and blowing the smoke onto the wall if necessary. If the smoke bounces off any section of wall, go over that area again, pushing the smoke into the wall with the action of the smudge stick and with your intention. Keep going over that section until the smoke is absorbed, as well as drawing one or more Lemniscates on that spot. These areas usually indicate negative psychic or emotional energies.

8. Put a Lemniscate in the middle of each wall, and over mirrors, windows and any shiny or glassy surface (especially black glass). If you're doing an especially large area, you may need to use an extra-large smudge stick or multiple sticks.
9. When you arrive back at your starting point, put a second Lemniscate over your first one to tie it off (completes the cleansing).

ADDITIONAL NOTES ON HOUSE AND AREA CLEANSINGS

- If you are cleansing a large house, you may need multiple smudge sticks. You can light a new smudge stick from the original smudge stick without having to recharge the new stick.
- If you want to do a very thorough cleansing, make sure to smoke all cupboards, closets, nooks, crannies, and shelves. Treat walk-in closets as small rooms.
- Be sure to carefully smoke and Lemniscate all mirrored and glass surfaces. Mirrors and windows are doorways that allow beings to penetrate your shields through the reflection. Black mirrors, in particular, are accesses to all worlds. Don't worry about the "why" of black mirrors or glass surfaces

for now… just be sure to smoke and Lemniscate all mirrored and glass surfaces.

- Treat all doors as walls. If you come to an open door, smoke the side of the door closest to you, then go around the back of the door and smoke that. Then move down the wall that is contiguous to the back of the door. If you come to a door that leads outside the house, treat the inside of the door as a wall and don't do the back (outside face) of the door.
- If you are cleansing an area only, shut all the doors to that area and treat the doors as walls. If you have an opening that has no door, draw a Lemniscate across the center of the open space.

CLEANSING OBJECTS AND PEOPLE WITH THE TWO ELEMENT CLEANSING RITUAL

- To cleanse any object, simply specify the object or use the phrase "these objects" instead of "these walls" in the charge verse. Hold the object in the column of smoke until the smoke clings to the object. Smoke will bounce off objects with especially "junky" energies, so keep holding the object in the column of smoke until the smoke is sticking easily to the object.

- It can be useful to cleanse a person, especially if they are suffering from an illness or conditions that seem to have mysterious origins or causes. To cleanse another person, charge the smudge stick using "Cleanse this person and cleanse his/her space." Start at the person's feet and begin smoking them, moving around them in a clockwise fashion (to the left) in an upward spiral that goes up over their head.
- Gently blow the smoke from the smudge stick onto the person's body, looking for places where the smoke does not stick. If you find such an area, keep blowing smoke over that area until the smoke sticks. You can also draw one or more Lemniscates on that spot. As you pass the person's face, have them inhale a breath of the smoke to cleanse the lining of the throat and lungs, since those are continuations of the outer skin.

To cleanse yourself, place the smudge stick on a fire-proof plate on the floor and be sure that the stick is generating a thick dense column of smoke. Then stand over the smudge stick with one foot on either side and weave back and forth slightly so that the smoke bathes you front and back. This works if you are clothed, but is more effective when you're nude. Yes, naked!

10.3

Simple Rituals and Spells

Witchcraft Command to Stop Panic Attacks and Other Negative States

This is one of easiest rituals in this book, as well as being one of the most fun. In this ritual you get to boss yourself around... and all you need for this ritual is a mirror!

If you are person who does not like to be told what to do by other people, then this magic ritual is custom-made for you. The goal of this ritual is to get you out of negative states by getting back into the present... the here and now.

How to Do This Ritual for Getting Into the Moment

All kinds of spiritual traditions tell us that to be happy and balanced we need to live in the present moment. Yet when we are in pain it can be difficult to focus on the present. Pain is, well, painful, and we often feel the need to escape it in some way.

The counterintuitive aspect of panic or negative emotions is that when we are in the present, our negativity becomes less painful and we become more aware of what is causing the problem. Becoming aware of and embracing the problem in the present moment can actually help lessen the uncomfortable sensations we experience.

The good news is that it's pretty simple to get back to present moment. Just follow these steps:

1. Find a mirror and stand in front of it. Any mirror will do, including a mirror hanging on the wall, your car's side-view mirror, or even a hand mirror.

2. Once you are in front of your mirror, look yourself directly in the eyes. Stare deeply into your eyes without blinking or looking away. Put all your focus into your eyes.

3. Speak to your image aloud in a voice of command. Using a voice of command and authority, order yourself, "Come to present time!" Be sure to put the full force of your intention behind the command.

4. Pause for a moment and become aware of your state. Do you feel less negative, less physically painful, less mentally nuts? If so, good. If not, repeat this ritual again.

You may have to do this ritual many times before all parts of yourself (mind, body, Spirit) decide to come to present time... and stay here. Don't worry if a lot of repetition is called for. Just keep repeating the ritual until you feel sane again.

The good news about repeating this ritual is that all levels of your being get a lot practice coming back to present time. That means the next time you use this simple ritual to order yourself back into present time, all parts of you are more likely to "snap back" to the present more quickly and easily. Once you are back in the present, you can use the other rituals in this book to change your state of being on a more permanent basis.

Practitioners of witchcraft and magic use this ritual often, both on themselves and on other people. This ritual is a command that body, mind and Spirit recognize and obey.

You can also use this technique with other people who are spiraling out of control. Instead of putting them in front of a mirror, you act as their mirror. Look deep into their eyes, just as you looked deep into your own eyes when you used this ritual on yourself. Once you have made eye contact, give them the command, "Come to present time." They will snap back into the moment. Just remember that you may need to repeat this command multiple times to keep the other person focused in present time.

WHY DOES THIS RITUAL WORK?

This ritual is all about commanding various parts of yourself to return to the present moment. When this ritual is done correctly and repeatedly, it works without fail. If you do not understand why this ritual works to move you out of any negative or "nutty" state, consider this:

> ***Any form of negativity exists in the past or the future.***

Think about it. When you feel nuts, what is really happening? You are doing one of two things. You are:

- reliving past negative events that have already happened
- projecting about future negative events you fear may occur

If you don't believe this, just think back to the last argument you had with someone. What was the *real* content of the argument about? While there may have been a present-time event that triggered the argument, the stuff that gets brought up is usually a rehash of old history, right?

Do lines like, "You always do that!" or "Oh, I can see this is going to turn out just like xxx did back in 2007!" sound familiar? Present time events pull in memories of past events, and that is what the argument is really about.

Conversely, the argument can be about future events. For instance, let's say you get an unexpected bill in the mail. All of sudden you start projecting out into the future about fearful events, like not being able to pay the bill. An argument begins. While the bill exists in present time, the argument is about a projected future.

Thus, it is simple common sense, not to mention a magical principle—that all negativity exists in the past or future, not in the present.

THE RUBBER BAND ALTERNATIVE TO THIS RITUAL

What should you do if you often become negative at work or in public places? You may not be able to run to the bathroom mirror multiple times per day to do this ritual. You can always use a rubber band as a reminder to come to present time. You can also use your smart phone. It just depends on whether you want to go low-tech or high-tech.

Using the rubber band instead of a mirror for this ritual is simple. Just wear a rubber band around your wrist at all times (or use a decorative elastic bracelet if that works better for you). When you feel yourself becoming negative, simply snap the rubber band around your wrist while saying to yourself in a quiet but forceful voice, "Come to present time!"

The slightly stinging sensation of the rubber band on your wrist will bring you back to present time, since all physical sensation exists in the present. To experience that sensation you have to come back to present time. You can sub-vocalize this command so that only you can hear it, but be sure to say the command aloud. In addition, put all of your intention behind the command. Your intention is just as important as the command!

Another option is to set your smart phone alarm to alert you multiple times a day. Whenever your smart phone alerts you, check whether you are feeling negative. If you are, use the rubber band ritual described earlier to bring yourself back to present time... and back to a more positive state!

One of our students came up with an even classier option to the rubber band. She wanted a ritual with a little more pizzazz to it, a little more style. She favored the angel Gabriel, so she created a ritual that included him. She found a charming but subtle pendant representing the angel Gabriel, and she wears it on a necklace.

When her pager buzzes her, instead of snapping a rubber band around her wrist, she reaches up and fingers the pendant, a gesture that appears natural and doesn't seem out of place, even in a boardroom. Lots of people fidget or have nervous habits, and when she reaches up to hold her pendant, it looks just like any other subconscious fidget. The ritual has worked, literally "like a charm," and brings her back to the here and now several times a day. She reports feeling more relaxed and at ease during the work day, and less tired at the end of the day.

10.4

Simple Rituals and Spells

Left Hand, Right Hand Ritual to Get Answers You Need

You are probably familiar with the saying the left hand does not know what the right is doing. Normally this phrase is used in a negative context—to criticize the government, for instance, or to imply that two people are not "on the same page." However, in a witchcraft practice, the fact that your left and right hands are often unaware of each other is a really good thing! You can use this disconnection between your hands, which is really a disconnection between mind and Spirit, to get some much-needed answers from your higher self!

USE YOUR RIGHT TO ASK THE UNIVERSE FOR INFORMATION

As a planetary citizen you have the right to ask the Universe for any information you choose. With enough experience with a witchcraft or magical practice, you can even access some or all of the information stored in the Akashic Records (the records of Universal history). So if you need information from the Universe, ask away!

Whether you need to locate hidden or inaccessible information, or you simply need some spiritual guidance or help from higher powers and beings, you have the right to ask. The good news is that there are plenty of powers and beings willing to help you get what you need. What you do with the information, especially if it relates to other people, is governed by Rules of the Road (see the beginning of this book for the Rules).

Accessing spiritual information, whether from your Spirit or from higher powers and beings, can ease your journey on life's rocky road. You are not "cheating" by getting help from higher powers and beings. In fact, getting in touch with Spirit and spiritual beings is one of the most primary of human lessons. The more you ask for help and information from angels, guides, animal totems, or your own Spirit the easier and more enjoyable your daily life will become.

There are several keys to working with your Spirit or powers and beings to get the information you need:

- Don't be afraid to ask—you're entitled to access any information in the Universe.
- Always thank your Spirit or your guides as soon as you ask for the information, before you get the information.
- Ask for the information to arrive in a way that you can easily understand.
- If you don't get the information you need the first time around, thank your source and ask for clarification. Don't be afraid to keep asking until you get what you want.
- Getting the information you want doesn't have to be difficult and arduous—the more you practice this process, the easier it will get.
- Don't second guess the information you get. Accept it with gratitude!

WHAT YOU WILL NEED FOR THE LEFT HAND, RIGHT HAND RITUAL

- a Sun Yellow candle
- wooden or paper matches (no lighters)
- a compass to find the cardinal direction East
- pen and paper (either a journal or book of shadows dedicated to rituals)

HOW TO DO THE LEFT HAND, RIGHT HAND RITUAL

Now that you know about your rights as a planetary citizen to access Universal information, let's get down to the details of this ritual. The Left Hand, Right Hand ritual makes you a channel for the information you need. In this ritual, you ask yourself one or more questions with your dominant hand, and then you answer those questions with your other hand. Follow these directions to perform this ritual:

1. Use your compass to determine the location of the cardinal direction East. While most rituals and spells are done sitting in the South facing North, this ritual is done sitting in the East facing West. This is

because East is the direction of knowledge and communication. This ritual is all about communication, making East the perfect direction from which to conduct this ritual.

2. Seat yourself comfortably in the East facing West. Place all the items you will need for this ritual on a table in front of you.

3. Light and charge the candle with the Sun Candle Blessing ritual (as taught earlier in this book). Wait until the Sun Candle has a tall working flame before proceeding.

4. Determine which hand is your dominant hand. The hand with which you write is usually your dominant hand, but if you are not sure (or you are ambidextrous) simply point to something. Whichever hand you used for pointing is you dominant hand. This may or may not be the hand with which you write.

5. Now write the question to which you seek the answer with your dominant hand. For instance, if you want to know what lesson you are to learn from a current traumatic experience, you might write the following question (on a sheet of paper or in your journal) with your dominant hand: "What lesson am I to learn from [briefly describe your current situation]?"

6. Then, with your other hand, write the answer. While you may not be used to writing with this hand, don't worry. Just scribble along as best you can, but be sure that you take enough time that the writing is legible.

> The key to this ritual is not to think about the answer. Just write the first thing your hand feels inspired to write. You'll often be quite surprised at the answer.

If your answer doesn't make sense to you, don't try to force it to make sense. Just keep the answer in your consciousness for a few days and see what occurs. We often receive answers in small chunks, which make them easier to digest. The answer you write may be only partial, and other events and situations in your life may fill in the remaining pieces. In addition, feel free to repeat this ritual for as many days as needed.

Be patient and just enjoy the inevitable unfolding of knowledge and understanding. This ritual can demonstrate to us the true pleasure of waiting for the knowledge we seek. The unfolding process will always be in perfect timing with our ability to process and use it.

10.5
SIMPLE RITUALS AND SPELLS

SPLIT PAPER DRILL TO UNLOAD "LOADED" ISSUES

Do you have a "loaded" issue in your life that has been bothering you for a long time? If so, here is a truly counter-intuitive but effective ritual that can help you unload the significance on the issue. When you unload the significance from an issue that has been bothering you, the issue will cease to bother you.

The reason a "loaded" issue bothers you is because both sides of the issue are heavy with forceful energy, as well as being in direct conflict with each other. Some practitioners call this situation a "must win/can't win." The Split Paper Drill is a spell that basically clears both sides of any issue so that there is no longer any conflict.

WHAT YOU WILL NEED FOR THE SPLIT PAPER DRILL RITUAL

- a Sun Candle
- paper or wooden matches
- a compass
- pen
- a stack of blank paper at least 8.5" x 11" in size
- a printed copy of the three charts following (photocopy from book or download a PDF at www.esotericschool.com/charts-split-paper-drill-ritual.pdf)

What is IMPORTANT about taking this job offer?	**What is NOT important about taking this job offer?**
1.	**1.**
What else is IMPORTANT about taking this job offer?	**What else is NOT important about taking this job offer?**
2.	**2.**
3.	**3.**
4.	**4.**
5.	**5.**

What is IMPORTANT about staying in my body?	What is NOT important about staying in my body?
1.	1.
What else is IMPORTANT about staying in my body?	What else is NOT important about staying in my body?
2.	2.
3.	3.
4.	4.
5.	5.

What is IMPORTANT about my spouse's infidelity?	What is NOT important about my spouse's infidelity?
1.	1.
What else is IMPORTANT about my spouse's infidelity?	What else is NOT important about my spouse's infidelity?
2.	2.
3.	3.
4.	4.
5.	5.

HOW TO DO THE SPLIT PAPER DRILL

While this ritual may appear to be similar to the Left Hand, Right Hand ritual—in which the goal is to gather information—in actuality the goal of this ritual is quite different. The aim of the Split Paper Drill ritual is to unload the Fire energy from the two sides of a loaded issue. This ritual is fairly simple, but does require quite a bit of repetition, so be patient with the process. Follow these steps to do this ritual:

1. Use your compass to determine the location of the cardinal direction East. As with the Left Hand, Right Hand ritual, this one is done sitting in the East facing West.

2. Seat yourself comfortably in the East facing West. Place all the items you will need for this ritual on a table in front of you.

3. Light and charge the candle with the Sun Candle Blessing ritual (as taught earlier in this book). Wait until the Sun Candle has a tall working flame before proceeding.

4. Copy one of the three charts you printed onto one of your sheets of blank paper. The questions provided in the sample charts are merely examples. Fill in your own questions relating to the issue you wish to unload. You will notice that the sample charts contain questions relating to everything from practical matters (whether to take a job) to spiritual matters (how to stay in one's body). As you write your own questions, be sure to capitalize the words "IMPORTANT" and "NOT" exactly as shown in the sample charts. You may wish to add more lines to your chart, even expanding the chart to several additional pages. This will save time later, should you need the extra lines.

5. Before beginning this ritual, read through these notes. They will help you get the most out of this ritual:

   - You will be asking yourself the questions listed in the chart out loud. Don't doubt or negate whatever response you get when you ask. Just note it on the paper as an answer to the question from your mind's viewpoint.

   - It is not part of the ritual to attempt to evaluate any of the responses for logic, reasonableness, or relevance to the question that you asked. According to the mind, whatever the response is, it is logical and relevant. You don't have enough information to judge. You're not trying to figure out what any of this means.

   - If you begin giggling or laughing compulsively at any point, let it happen and do not block it. This is a manifestation of having released something of great emotional importance relative to the issue being worked on, and you're clearing that energy out.

   - If working on a particular column, say the first one, and in going down the page you should produce a strong emotional reaction, such as anger, or a feeling of frustration, wanting to tear up your paper, fear, feeling jittery, being easily distracted by noises or other thoughts, grief or sadness, or feelings of sudden tiredness or sleepiness, immediately work on the other column of the pair until you feel better. If you are working on the left side and get these responses, go to the right side until you feel better (as many times as you need to, even if it takes 10 to 15 or more askings of that same question. Just keep doing it, even if you've already done that side until you feel OK again. And then return to the column that was giving you trouble.

6. Once you thoroughly understand the notes about this exercise, proceed with the ritual by asking yourself aloud the question in the top left box. As you do so, emphasize the word "IMPORTANT."

7. Write down the first thing coming up in response, whether it's a picture, a word, a feeling, a voice in the head, a body sensation, a memory, or anything else. Once you have written your answer on the paper, acknowledge your response by telling yourself, "Thank you" or "Good" or "Excellent." This helps to acknowledge and appreciate your mind's response.

8. Ask yourself the same question from the left column aloud, again emphasizing the word "IMPORTANT." Again write down the first thing that comes to you as a response. Remember to acknowledge your answer each time with a "Good" or "Thanks."

9. Keep asking yourself the same question in the left column until you have six total answers in the left column. Then move to the right hand column. Remember that if, at any time, you get a strong

emotional response (such as anger, grief, fear, or any other of the emotions listed earlier) you should switch to the other column regardless of how many answers you have in the current column.

10. Once you move to the right column, follow the same procedure. Ask yourself aloud the question in the upper right box of the chart, this time emphasizing the word "NOT."

11. Write down the first response, whether it's a picture, a word, a feeling, a voice in the head, a body sensation, a memory, or anything else. Remember to acknowledge your answer each time with a "Thank You" or "Excellent."

12. Ask yourself the same question in the right column aloud, again emphasizing the word "NOT." Again write down the first thing that comes to you as a response. Keep asking until you have at least 6 items in the right column. Remember that if, at any time, you get a strong emotional response (such as anger, grief, fear, or any other of the emotions listed earlier) you should switch to the other column regardless of how many answers you have in the current column.

13. Now switch back to the left column and start with the question in that column, such as, "What is IMPORTANT about...?"

We suggest that you do this ritual for 15 to 30 minutes per day. Plan on doing this ritual for many days in a row, depending on how "loaded" is the issue you are handling with this ritual.

Don't assume if you get the same answers for several days that you will continue to get the same answers indefinitely.

Just keep doing the ritual. One of the things that this repetition does is that it levels the significance on both sides of the "loaded" issue. It is extremely helpful because once you know how to do this, it balances out uneven significance that you have placed on things, and it will free you up.

You will feel differently about the loaded issues when this ritual has had its intended effect. Once the significances on both sides of the issue have been unloaded, you will see the issue with much more clarity. You will then be able to make clear conscious decisions, as well as act with power and authority. You will no longer feel confused about the issue, nor will you keep "changing your mind" about a particular decision.

You may, as with many other rituals in this book, do this ritual for 40 days in a row. Yes, we know, it sounds like a lot of monotonous work. However, based on our experience with our students, we know that this exercise can have profound life-changing effects when done persistently, consistently, and correctly. Remember that magic is a precision science so follow the instructions closely. Take your time, think it through, and do it right… just make sure you *do* it!

10.6

Simple Rituals and Spells

Simple Question Circle to Get the Answers You Need

In these uncertain times people are actively seeking answers to problems ranging from job loss to foreclosure. If you need some spiritual guidance from powers and beings, a question circle may be just the ticket for you.

A question circle is a witchcraft ritual in which you ask for help and guidance from the Winds of the four directions. There is no visible circle in a question circle. The circle is formed by the path connecting the four cardinal directions of East, South, West, and North. During the question circle ritual, you will walk to each direction, this forming a "circle."

Simple Question Circle to Get the Answers You Need

The question circle is a satisfying ritual and you only need a few tools. One of the best aspects of the question circle ritual is that, because you are asking for guidance from four *different* directions, you will get four different perspectives or answers on your question.

In addition, this ritual is a ***contact ritual,*** which means that you will be making contact with higher powers and beings. Repeated contact with such beings, along with regularly expressed appreciation, will lead to a lasting relationship with these higher beings. Once you have developed a more solid relationship with these beings, you will be able to ask them for guidance more quickly and easily as time passes.

What You Will Need for the Question Circle Ritual

- a Sun Candle
- paper or wooden matches
- a compass
- pen and paper (or a journal or your book of shadows)

PREPARING YOURSELF FOR A QUESTION CIRCLE

Before you begin your question circle ritual you will need to prepare yourself. Be prepared for a flurry of information from each and every direction. The information usually comes faster than you can write—just keep up as well as you can, making shorthand notes where possible.

As you ask your question to each direction, keep writing until the flow of information stops. Each direction will give you different types of information.

For instance, the East will give you information about communication, planning, and ideas. The South will give you guidance on action steps, will, power, energy, and desire. The West will give you feelings and spiritual guidance, while the North will give you practical steps. Enjoy the variety of answers that will come flooding to you!

HOW TO DO THE QUESTION CIRCLE RITUAL

Once you have gathered your materials and prepared yourself, then you are ready to do the question circle ritual. Simply follow these steps:

1. Sit in the center of the circle facing East. Light and charge your Sun Candle. Then write your question in your journal or book of shadows. For instance, you might write, "What's the best way to get a job?" or "How can I best find my soul mate?" or "What lesson do I need to learn from the life-threatening illness that has come into my life?"

   Now contemplate your question for three to five minutes, letting the question sit in your mind without trying to answer it. Once you feel a sense of peace, quiet, and curiosity about your question, proceed to the next step.

2. Bring your Sun Candle, pen, and journal to the East quarter of your circle. Sit facing the outside of the circle (facing East). Ask the Winds of Knowledge what you need to know about your situation. For instance, you may say aloud, "Winds of Knowledge, please offer me guidance on [*fill in the blank you're your question*]. Thank you in advance for your help on this issue."

   As is true when requesting help from all higher powers and beings, always express your appreciation and gratitude immediately after your request. Now become very quiet inside and wait for the Winds of

Knowledge to answer you. Be prepared to write down everything that comes to you. Don't think about it, just write. You may hear the answer as your own voice in your own mind. Don't worry—that's perfectly natural. Keep writing until you no longer receive information. Thank the Winds of Knowledge, and then move to the next step.

3. Move to the South, and sit facing South (the outside of the circle). Ask the Winds of Power to show you what actions you need to take for your situation, using a question formed similarly to the one you used to ask the Winds of Knowledge for help. Remember to thank the Winds of Power immediately after you make your request. Again, write any answers that come to you. Thank the Winds of Power again afterward.

4. Move to the next quarter, in the West, and sit facing West. Ask the Winds of Feeling what emotional shifts you need to make regarding your situation. In addition, you may want to ask for spiritual enlightenment. Thank the Winds of Feeling immediately after you make your request, as well as after you have received the requested information.

5. Move to the North, and sit facing North. Ask the Winds of Strength how you can build a foundation for the future you want. Ask for practical guidance about your situation. Thank the Winds of Strength before and after the requested information is delivered. Remember to keep writing—don't stop to worry about whether the information is right or wrong. You won't have time for doubt if you want

to capture all the information from each of the directions.

6. Finally, move back to the center of your circle and sit facing East. Thank the Winds of the four directions for their help regarding your question. Read through the answers that have come to you from each direction. Slowly digest the information. You may want to repeat the question circle several times, at different times or on different days, until you get clarity on your situation. The Winds never mind being asked repeatedly for clarification.

10.7

Simple Rituals and Spells

Grounding Out Negative Energies with Grandmother's Tears

Negative energy is something that can be dealt with through a variety of magic or witchcraft rituals. Using magical stones is a good way to ground out these unwanted energies.

One stone in particular, called Grandmother's Tears or Apache Tears, is very effective at grounding out any excessive energy you no longer want. This stone is a special form of obsidian (volcanic black glass) made of feldspar, hornblend, biotite, and quartz.

Grounding Out Negative Energies with Grandmother's Tears

This stone looks opaque black in ordinary light, but appears translucent when held up to strong light. These stones have actually been spewed out from past volcanic explosions, and can be found in and around Superior, AZ.

These stones are effective for grounding out excess or negative energies including anger, frustration, pain, or plain irritation. Grounding out these energies into Grandmother's Tears allows you to safely transfer these unwanted energies into the half worlds (a safe place for negative energies).

Tribal people have been using these stones for generations for this purpose. Many practitioners use crystals for various types of healing work. However, crystals—and in particular quartz crystals—are easily contaminated, and need to be magically cleansed quite frequently.

Because Grandmother's Tears do not actually "hold" energies transferred into them, but instead send those energies into the half worlds, these stones do not need to be cleansed unless desired by the practitioner. The stone acts as a portal to the half worlds, and none of that energy will come back to you.

You can find Grandmother's Tears in most gem stores and in online stores.

HOW TO GROUND OUT NEGATIVE ENERGIES WITH A GRANDMOTHER'S TEAR

The ritual of flowing negative energy into a Grandmother's Tear stone is so easy that it can and should be used as many times as necessary daily. Follow these steps to do this ritual:

1. Figure out whether your left or right hand is your dominant hand by simply pointing at an object in your vicinity. Whichever hand you used to point is your dominant hand.

2. Hold the Grandmother's Tear stone in your dominant hand. Use your intention to flow any unwanted energy into the stone, knowing that the energy will go straight into the half worlds, and will not "bounce back" to you. If you need help "flowing," just bring up every thought, feeling, or physical sensation related to the issue that is bothering you. Use your intention to "push" all these into the stone.

3. When you feel a sense of calm or peace, you may stop flowing energy into the stone. Alternately, the stone may feel warm, heavy, charged, or loaded. At that point, you know that your flowing is complete. Stop flowing and simply breathe, relax, and enjoy the sense of peace.

CARRYING OR STORING YOUR GRANDMOTHER'S TEARS

Some people like to carry a Grandmother's Tear stone around with them. You can easily tuck one into your pocket so you can access it whenever you need to flow negative energy.

Alternately, some women wear small versions of these stones as pendants on a necklace. If you choose this method, be sure to use a silver chain, since gold is magically a much less stable metal.

Other people buy multiple stones and keep them available everywhere—in the car, in the kitchen, next to the phone, and on their desks! All of these techniques work. Just pick the method that fits your personality best.

If you ever need to store your stones, the safest way to store them is in a pewter box. Pewter is a metal that has protective magical properties. Pewter protects anything stored from negative energy, and pewter boxes are especially useful for other types of stones, such as crystals, which tend to pick up all kinds of energies with ease.

If for any reason your Grandmother's Tear stone start to feel "junky" or overloaded with energy, you can cleanse it several different ways. While this rarely happens to Grandmother's Tears stones, some practitioners prefer to cleanse their stones monthly, just to ensure safety. Two of the easiest ways to cleanse your Grandmother's Tear stone are:

- hold it in the smoke of a charged cedar/sage smudge stick (see previous instructions on how to charge a smudge stick in the section called *Relocating Unwanted Spirits Away from Your Home*)
- bury the stone in the Earth for a Moon cycle (Mother Earth takes care of all kinds of energies, and is a great magical cleanser!).

10.8

SIMPLE RITUALS AND SPELLS

PREVENT NIGHTMARES WITH MAGICAL WATER

If you or a loved one is having problems with nightmares, there is a simple ritual that uses a glass of water to prevent them. With this ritual you can effortlessly use standing water to magically clear negative energy and prevent nightmares.

Water is the element of the Spirit, and works well to soak up the terrors of the Spirit as well. A simple remedy for nightmares is simply to place a full glass of magically programmed water on your nightstand before bed. The water will absorb any negative spiritual energy during the night, and helps prevent nightmares for some people.

WHAT YOU WILL NEED FOR THE MAGICAL WATER RITUAL

- a Sun Candle
- paper or wooden matches
- a compass
- a glass, preferably bright blue in color
- spring water
- sea salt

HOW TO PREVENT NIGHTMARES WITH THE MAGICAL WATER RITUAL

To prevent nightmares with a glass of water, you will need to program the glass of water each night. Follow these steps to perform this ritual:

1. Use your compass to locate the cardinal direction West. Since nightmares are "terrors of the Spirit," and West is the direction of the Spirit, this ritual is done sitting in and facing West.

2. Charge the Sun Candle and wait until it is burning with a tall working flame.

3. Pick up the glass of water, fill the cup halfway with spring water, and add a sprinkling of sea salt.

4. Cup the glass it in both of your hands. As you hold the glass, flow Water Blue (bright blue) energy through the glass in a clockwise direction, from left hand to right hand, through the glass. Do this for 30 seconds or so. Don't think about this process—just do it!

5. Now swirl the water in the glass gently in a clockwise direction. Breathe Water Blue (bright blue) energy into the glass of water.

6. Say the following verse aloud in a voice of command, blowing Water Blue energy into the glass before and after the verse, as well as between each line of the verse. Continue to swirl the water gently in the glass in a clockwise direction as you say the verse. This verse "charges" or programs the Water to prevent nightmares.

   Water and Earth where you stand,

   Let no spell nor adverse purpose land,

   Not in accord with me.

   Keep nightmares far from this space,

   Far from here send baneful trace.

   Thus my will, so it be!

7. Once the glass of water has been "charged," place it on the nightstand next to the affected person's head. Blow out the Sun Candle and store it.

   During the night, the "charged" water will absorb any thoughts and emotions released during the night. In addition, the charged water will keep nightmares from outside sources at bay. During sleep, the affected person is more spiritually open, which allows the standing water to more easily absorb the negative energies that cause nightmares.

8. In the morning, dump the water from the glass down the drain. *Never* drink this water, as it is filled with negative energy and you will just reabsorb all the energies you released during the night. Many people find that using this technique 40 nights in a row is an effective way to clear negative energies and prevent nightmares on a more permanent basis.

OTHER MAGICAL METHODS TO PREVENT NIGHTMARES

While we have found that the magic water ritual is very effective at preventing nightmares, we have also found that these four following methods are useful for some people.

If you suffer from nightmares and can't sleep at night because of them, you may wish to try the magic water ritual first, and then also try these four other rituals.

These rituals are a big part of many tribal traditions and have worked for many suffering sleepless nights because of nightmares.

1. SUN CANDLE

   Light and charge a Sun Candle following the procedure outlined earlier in this book. A Sun Yellow candle encased in glass and set on a plate is your safest option. Let the candle burn all night, if necessary. Sun Yellow nourishes your Spirit and keeps your energetic vibrations high and light while you sleep.

2. ESSENTIAL OILS

   Before bed, add a drop of soothing essential oils to your pillowcase or sheets, or rub them (mixed with a carrier oil, such as almond oil) on the bottoms of your feet, on your neck, or on your forehead. If you have a partner, trade essential oil foot rubs before bed. Calming and soothing essential oils that will help prevent nightmares include lavender, orange, rose, sandalwood, and frankincense.

3. DREAMCATCHERS

   Native Americans have long used dreamcatchers to prevent nightmares from intruding during the night. Made of leather and sinew, and often decorated with feathers, shells, stones, and symbols, dreamcatchers should be hung at the head of your bed or over your bed. They will "catch" nightmares, stopping them before they reach you. You can easily find dreamcatchers in many online stores.

4. FLOWER ESSENCES

   Mix up some flower essences to take during the day and before bed to prevent nightmares. Rock Rose is excellent for terrors, such as those that often appear in nightmares.

Aspen helps young children who suffer from nightmares. Mugwort helps keep dreams from interrupting your sleep, while White Chestnut works well for repetitive dreams that haunt. Star of Bethlehem is a great overall flower essence to ease fears and terrors. You can easily buy these flower essences in many online stores. Add four drops of each applicable essence to a bottle of pure spring water, and sip on the water all day, and right before bed.

10.9

SIMPLE RITUALS AND SPELLS

THROWING AWAY PSYCHIC GARBAGE (JUST A STONE'S THROW AWAY!)

At a seminar on healing we once heard a woman tell of an exercise that relieved her of her troubles. She said she walked around a large park with a canvas sack. For every problem in her life, she picked up a big rock, associated it with the problem, and put the rock in her sack. She said that by the time she had finished putting all the rocks in her sack, she could hardly carry or drag it around—that's how many problems she had been carrying around with her.

Throwing Away Psychic Garbage (Just a Stone's Throw Away!)

When she was done, she dragged her sack over to a lake in the park. She then took each rock out of the sack one by one and, saying "Goodbye," heaved each rock as far as she could into the lake. At the end of the entire process, she left the park with an empty sack and a very light heart.

Does Her Method Have a Basis in Witchcraft or Magic?

Her story was so inspiring and wonderful that we began thinking about the magical basis for her method—and discovered that it was actually valid and useful. Her method falls under the category of simulacra magic, in which physical objects are used to represent a person, place, or thing in life. Once you correlate the physical object to the person, place, or thing in life, what you do to the object you also do to the person, place, or thing.

A simulacrum is a likeness (simulacra is the plural of simulacrum). Using simulacra in magical operations is very similar to classic voodoo, where you associate or "key" an object to a person or thing. Whatever you do magically or otherwise to the object also happens to the person or thing it is keyed to. Simulacra allow you to perform magical operations on people or things even if they are located thousands of miles away. Most of the spell work we have done to date is Air and Fire magic. Simulacra are Water and Earth magic.

For instance, to keep a space station from falling out of the sky, you could buy a model of it, key it, and do magic on it. You can use photographs, pictures, dolls, small models, lists, symbols, Tarot layouts, and other objects as simulacra.

One of the teachers at the Church of Seven Arrows did something magical to blur herself in a photograph because she knew that pictures could be used as simulacra. You can also use chess pieces or objects made of stone, ceramic, wood or glass. If you use wood be sure it is fairly dense otherwise it will not easily key. Plastic and rubber do not key well so don't use them.

According to the Law of Similarity, the greater the likeness (between a simulacra and what it is keyed to) the greater the resonance or connection. Photographs and pictures have a great likeness to the original subjects, so they already access the original subjects. All you have to do is key them (we will teach you how to key in a later section).

Using simulacra allows you to do magical procedures on people and things you are not in direct physical contact with. In fact the person you affect can be all the way on the other side of the world, or you can affect a global situation. Refer to Rules of the Road before performing simulacra magic to ensure you don't suffer from side-bands or backlash.

In this case, using simulacra magic allows you to safely handle and get rid of negative energies in your life. By making a psychic connection between the rock and the negative emotion or situation, you can perform a magical procedure to get rid of the negative energy.

Note: As with all spell work, record everything in your Book of Shadows. Also remember that magic is a precision science and altered procedures produce altered results!

What the woman did with her rocks was to create a correlation or psychic connection between a rock and a problem in her life. This process is called "keying." When she threw each rock into the lake, she severed her physical connection to the rock and, by the laws of simulacra magic, also her connection to her problem.

Keying magical tools is a process that:

1. Clears out junky or impure energies.
2. Attunes the tool to the user which makes the tool incompatible to other people.
3. Aligns the molecules in the tool so that the energies flow only in certain directions.
4. Associates certain objects with people, places, or things (although in this book we *never* encourage you to key objects with people, since this is an act of advanced magic and the chance of breaking Rules of the Road is high).

HOW TO THROW YOUR TROUBLES AWAY!

As you have probably figured out by now, the ritual used by the woman in the earlier story is both simple and effective. Plus, the ritual does have a sound basis in witchcraft and magic. So here's how you do this simple ritual:

1. Bring a sack to a park that has nice smooth river stones and a large body of water (be sure the sack will be large enough to hold a single stone for every problem you want to throw out of your life!).

2. As you walk through the park, look for stones that call to you.

3. Pick up any stone that attracts your attention (avoid huge stones or you will never be able to drag your sack to the water!).

4. As you hold the stone in your dominant hand (the hand with which you point), think of problem with which you want to "key" the stone. Then key the stone to the problem by bringing up every thought, feeling, or physical sensation related to the issue to be keyed. Use your intention to "push" all these into the stone. Be careful *never* to key a stone to a person or live being. You can key stones to situations, but never the people involved in the situation.

5. Once the stone feels heavy, loaded, tingly, or warm, you know the stone is keyed. Put the stone in the sack.

6. Move on to the next stone and repeat the process.

7. Once you have "keyed" enough stones for your own satisfaction, drag your sack of stones to the body of

water. Remember, you can repeat this ritual at any time, so you don't have to key a stone for *every* problem in your life right now. Just do enough to satisfy yourself.

8. Once at the water, pick each stone out of the sack. Hold the stone briefly, and then toss it with all your might into the water. This physical disconnection will sever the issue from your life. IF you want, you can also say the disconnect litany in a voice of command before launching each stone into the water:

   I am neither your creature nor your get,

   To be moved by your whim or your let;

   I will go my own way,

   By night or by day,

   To serve my own purposes yet.

9. Once your sack is empty, your ritual is complete. Consider yourself having "paid into your practice" and know that your practice will pay you back. Not only that, but you will undoubtedly have a warm sense of satisfaction having released all that negativity from your life!

10.10

Simple Rituals and Spells

Simple Candle Spell with Directors and Limiters

The big secret of getting help from the Universe isn't a big secret at all. The Universe already knows that you need help... all you have to do is ask. And one of the best and most specific ways to ask for help from the Universe is to do a simple candle spell with directors and limiters.

WHAT IS A CANDLE SPELL?

The candle used in this simple candle spell is the Sun Candle that you have been using throughout this book. Specifically, a candle spell is a spell that programs one or more candles to act in accord with a spell's purpose, directors and limiters, and verses (although we will not be using verses in the simple candle spell we teach in this section).

The candles used in a candle spell energize, activate, and feed the spell as well as assisting in programming the spell. The candle also translates the directors and limiters into an actual energy matrix that has force in the world, as well as continually increasing the energy of the spell matrix.

Remember, a spell is a formalized intention, an actual energy form that overcomes obstacles to achieve a stated aim. Lighting a candle that is set on top of a set of directors and limiters puts the spell into motion.

WHAT ARE DIRECTORS AND LIMITERS?

Now we just need to teach you how to write directors and limiters. Directors and limiters are no big deal. Directors are what you want your spell to do. Limiters are what you do *not* want your spell to do (such as cause harm or death to someone).

Specifically, directors and limiters specify the what, how, and when factors of a spell. You always need to specify directors and limiters for candle and Tarot spells (we will cover only a simple candle spell in this book).

Directors and limiters program your simple candle spell in terms of:

- the purpose of the spell
- how certain elements and energies are to be used
- the safeguards on the spell
- when the spell will start and stop

Specify anything that is important in your directors and limiters. For instance, if you are writing a spell for a new job you may want to specify the job description, amount of pay, type of company you want to be involved with, what kinds of benefits are involved, when you want the new job to start, the type of boss you want, and so forth.

Anything you don't specify is left to chance and spells usually follow the path of least resistance. Without directors and limiters you may achieve your goal but the spell may use methods that are illegal, dangerous, or harmful to self and others. The directors and limiters should almost be legalese. Think the way a lawyer might think when working on a contract. You don't have to put anything in your directors and limiters that you will do yourself, such as research on property values before buying a piece of property.

One student developed and launched a spell for a new job without specifying in her directors and limiters that her salary come from legal means. She ended up with an ideal job, wonderful working conditions, and co-workers she loved. She had to quit the job, though, when she discovered that she was working for the Mafia.

If your spell involves other people be sure that the directors and limiters are not binding (i.e. taking away a person's choice or forcing them to do something against their will). If you feel that someone's attitudes will affect your spell, you can set up a limiter preventing that person's attitude from affecting the spell or invite powers and beings to help.

Do not try to modify that person's behavior by binding them. Avoid enforcers, which are factors that force you to live your life a certain way, in your directors and limiters. For instance, a student once specified that the Universe not bring him more business than he could emotionally handle. After he launched the spell he broke up with his girlfriend and became an emotional wreck. The Universe therefore sent him absolutely no business!

When specifying numbers in your directors and limiters (such as age, salary, size, etc.), use a range rather than a single number so that your spell has more freedom to achieve the goal. Also, make sure your directors are reasonable. One student asked for $10,000 to manifest immediately. This is not reasonable. A spell is an energy matrix that gathers force and overcomes barriers over time—it rarely works right away. If you ask for something impossible you nullify the spell immediately.

An Esoteric School teacher once did a Tarot spell to prevent a bill from passing that would stop the sale of all supplements. It had already passed in the Senate and had a majority in the House. It was coming through to finalization in the House. The teacher did the spell and for two years nothing happened. Then, the day that the bill came before the House, the congressman who proposed the bill pulled it. The spell actualized in a single hour, two years after it was launched! The moral of this story is to be patient!

In the beginning, design your spells to create relatively small effects over a fairly short period of time. As you gain experience you can increase the content and reach of your spells.

Use limiters to program start and stop perimeters into the spell. You can even specify a delayed starting time for the spell using a limiter. You may also want to put in a standard limiter that says, "No one shall suffer harm, untimely death, or loss of property as the result of this spell," or something similar. It blocks the spell from taking certain harmful pathways in achieving its goal.

SAMPLE DIRECTORS AND LIMITERS

To give you an idea of how to write directors and limiters, here are some examples to get you started!

MONEY SPELL – DIRECTORS AND LIMITERS

1. To bring at least $10,000.00 in four to five weeks, by September 1st, xxxx, and not more than one million dollars by December xxxx, although the upper limit-date may later be extended.
2. No harm shall come to anyone, nor untimely death, nor loss of property as a result of this spell.
3. Whatever money shall come as a result of this spell shall be free and clear, with no strings attached.

4. The money will be used to pay off debts, to start my new career, and to purchase a house.

5. The spell will be open to support, help, and empowerment from angels and higher beings that can make a positive contribution.

6. My attitudes and fears will not have an adverse affect on this spell.

HOUSE LOCATING SPELL, DIRECTORS AND LIMITERS

1. To locate a house available for rent in or near XXXX, Colorado – available for rent between the start of this spell and up through first week of May, xxxx.

2. House will have at least four bedrooms and two bathrooms (full baths), plus a large kitchen with a side-by-side refrigerator or space for same.

3. House will have at least a two-car garage and a yard at least as large as xxxxx, and/or larger.

4. House will be available at least for two years, and the rent will not exceed $x,xxx a month with no penalty for late payment.

5. The landlord is to be local and honest, cooperative, friendly, and open-minded.

6. Our dog will be welcome and the area will be safe for her, not close to a busy street.

7. The space will work well for my healing business, with no legal restrictions or attitudes that oppose that.

8. The property will be of a sacred and spiritual nature for harmonious living for all of us.

9. The spell will help xxxx and xxxx in their search and work well with powers and beings (allies).

SPELL TO INCREASE HEALING AND MASSAGE PRACTICE, DIRECTORS AND LIMITERS

1. One shift at xxxx per week

2. Four to six hours at xxxx

3. Three to fourteen hours a week private practice

4. No more than five treatments a day – five days a week

5. Yearly income: $40,000-$60,000

6. Referrals from current clients

7. Clients of decency who respect and appreciate my work

8. Clients dependable and willing to pay

9. Changes to occur within three to four months of spell initiation.

HOW TO DO A SIMPLE CANDLE SPELL WITH DIRECTORS AND LIMITERS

Now that you know the specific definitions of a candle spell, directors, and limiters, all that remains is to design and launch your simple candle spell. You need follow only three steps to do this spell: write, light, and be bright!

1. WRITE

First, write your directors and limiters as clearly and concisely as possible. Once you have written your directors and limiters, go back and re-read the previous section on how to write directors and limiters. Be sure that you are not violating Rules of Road. At the same time, you want to allow your spell plenty of space and time to work.

Write what you want as precisely as possible while still allowing the Universe some flexibility in delivering on your desires. For instance, if you need some money, write down a range of dates by which you would like for money to arrive. Write down a range of dollars, such as "between $1,000 and $2,000." Be sure to specify that the money should be "legally free and clear with no penalties" and that there should be no death or loss of property as a result of the Universe granting this request!

Take as much time as you need with this step because you want to get this part right. As George Dew would say, "Take your time, think it through, and do it right!"

2. LIGHT

Next, put the paper on which your directors and limiters are clearly printed on a plate under your Sun Yellow candle (you may wish to fold the paper to allow it to fit easily under the candle on the plate). Then proceed to charge your Sun Candle as you have with rituals throughout this book (sitting in the South facing North):

Child of Wonder,

Child of Flame,

Nourish My Spirit

And Bring My Aim!

You can repeat the phrase three to seven times if you like. Leave the candle burning for 30 to 60 minutes at a time. At the end of that time, blow out the candle. Blowing rather than snuffing the flame "sends" your request to the Universe. Repeat this ritual every single day for up to 40 days.

3. BE BRIGHT

While the Universe is working on delivering your request, your job (aside from doing the simple Sun Candle spell daily) is to be bright. In other words, keep an open mind and heart. Look for possible signs that your request is coming to you. Appreciate where you are. Avoid being a Doubting Thomas. Find as much peace and joy as you can find.

Be happy! The Universe has a much easier time delivering to a happy and joyful recipient. After all, one of our "jobs" on this planet is to "sound a joyous note to Creator's ear" (according to the Hopis). So you do your job of being bright after performing the ritual, and you will get help from the Universe without a doubt.

Amaze and surprise yourself by following these directions. Magic and witchcraft are real and they do work. Getting help from the Universe isn't difficult... and it's so much more fun than sitting on the pity pot!

On Love Spells

People ask us for help all the time with love spells. Unfortunately, the types of love spells that most people want to cast break Rules of the Road. Why? Because they "bind" other people. In other words most people want help casting a spell that will "force" a specific person to fall in love with them. Because this type of spell breaks Rules of the Road, it is certain to backfire.

The reason that love spells don't work is because they break one of the fundamental rules of magical practice, rule #2 in Rules of the Road, which says:

> ***Don't bind another being unless you are willing to be likewise bound. This applies to many love spells and some kinds of healing rituals.***

It is like the Golden Rule:

> ***Don't do unto others what you would not want them to do unto you.***

Think about this. Would you want someone that you don't really love to bind you and make you fall in love with them? Probably not. The same holds true in any binding love spell.

If the person of your dreams does not love you, then binding him or her with a love spell may cause him or her to pay attention to you in the short term, but the long-term backlash could get ugly. The problem is that you will have a hard time predicting what kind of karmic backlash would result from this kind of spell.

The good news is that you can still cast a love spell. You just need one of a different flavor. While you can't cast a spell to make a specific person fall for you, you *can* cast a spell to bring a person of your dreams into your life. To start this spell, you need to first write directors and limiters. These tell your spell what you want the spell to do (directors) and what you don't want the spell to do (limiters). For instance, your directors may say that you want to attract a man or woman who:

- is between the ages of 30 and 40
- lives within 100 miles of you
- has a steady job and earns between $x and $y annually
- shares similar interests as you (you might want to be specific here)
- has a certain kind of personality
- has any other desired characteristics

Your limiters may state that the man or woman:

- does not have any pre-existing health issues
- does not have any children from previous marriages
- any other limiters you do not want to bring into a new relationship

Obviously you may not be able to think of everything to put on your list of directors and limiters, but just try to focus on the most important factors. For instance, you may find a kind temperament (with no tendencies toward violence) to be of great importance. If so, add that to your list. Also, be sure to make any numbers in your list ranges, such as "earns an income between $x and $y." This gives the spell more room to work.

One other crucial point: the more specific your list of directors and limiters, the more force it will take to bring the love of your life to you. If you already feel a lot of resistance in the love-life department, you may want to start with a more general list and place fewer "demands" on your spell in the beginning.

As the spell begins to attract potential soul mates into your life, you can always go back and "tweak" the list until it brings you the exact right person. Love, like everything else in life, is sometimes a process. As our teacher Abraham-Hicks says,

> ***"You'll never get it done and you'll never get it wrong."***

Once you have written a solid set of directors and limiters, use the steps provided earlier to perform a simple candle spell. Most of all enjoy the process. The Universe would much prefer to deliver to a happy person than to a grumpy one!

MAGIC SPELLS IN BABY STEPS

When people have spell work problems, there are some common errors that occur over and over. One thing that happens on a regular basis with people who are not having success with magic spells is that they ignore a key magical principle crucial to a successful spell. It is this principle:

"A small change in the present creates a larger change in the future."

WHAT DOES A SMALL CHANGE MEAN IN A MAGIC SPELL?

When people first learn how to create and launch their own magic spells, they usually get so excited that they try to change the world overnight. We can tell you it's not going to happen. Magic can achieve a lot, but biting off more than you can chew can mean a failed spell.

So what does it mean to take baby steps when it comes to magic spells? It means casting a small spell, waiting to see a change, and then casting the next logical spell in the chain until you get to your desired result.

AN EXAMPLE OF A CHAIN OF MAGIC SPELLS

So here is an example. Let's say that you want to attract your soul mate into your life. You've been dating but haven't found the right person yet. In fact, all you've found are a bunch of the wrong people. Now you want to apply spell work to the problem. How would you take baby steps? Here's a series that might work for you:

1. ***Realize that your soul mate is out there.*** Nothing in the Universe is impossible. You may want to incorporate an affirmation related to this in your daily life or meditation.

2. ***Define your soul mate on paper.*** List all the qualities that you want and don't want in a soul mate. See the earlier section on *Love Spells* for more instructions on how to write directors and limiters to attract a soul mate. Put the list in a safe place to use later.

3. ***Law of Attraction tells us*** that if something isn't happening (like your soul mate has not shown up yet), that we are somehow blocking what we desire. Do some simple spell work to change yourself so that you are better able to attract your soul mate into your life.

Hire some angels, use some flower essences (for instance, Cayenne for rapid change, Walnut for life transitions, Mimulus if you have a specific fear of relationships), or choose some magic symbols that will break down your resistance. One gal listed all her barriers to a soul mate on a sheet of paper (including her general air of pessimism about the subject and her fear of rejection), then burned it every day for 40 days as part of her morning meditation. She was literally burning up her barriers to a solid relationship with her soul mate. This worked well for her, as she met and became engaged to her soul mate within three months.

4. ***Now pull out your "soul mate" directors and limiters list.*** Follow the directions given earlier on doing a simple candle spell with directors and limiters.

In other words, do lots of little rituals and spells, and allow the changes to happen over time. A small change in the present creates a larger change in the future. Each small magic spell or magical act you do will bring your soul mate closer to you.

Allow time between magical acts to let the spells take action. Allow the Universe to do the bulk of the work. Put your focus on relaxing and allowing between-times. Most of all, enjoy and anticipate the magical result that is on its way to you!

11

More Complex Rituals and Spells

Rituals and Spells Done With Magical Tools

11.1

MORE COMPLEX RITUALS AND SPELLS

MAGICAL APPLES (NOT SNOW WHITE'S!)

Using simulacra magic you can get rid of bad habits, lose weight, get rid of a bad debt, or even heal a tumor. In this section we will teach you how to use an apple to get rid of something unwanted in your life.

WHAT IS SIMULACRA MAGIC?

A simulacrum is a likeness (simulacra is the plural of simulacrum). Using simulacra in magical operations is very similar to classic voodoo, where you key an object to a person or thing. Whatever you do magically or otherwise to the object also happens to the person or thing it is keyed to. Simulacra allow you to perform magical operations on people or things even if they are located thousands of miles away. Simulacra magic falls into the area of Water and Earth spell work.

You can use photographs, pictures, dolls and other small models, lists, symbols, Tarot layouts, and other objects as simulacra. You can also use chess pieces or objects made of stone, ceramic, wood or glass. If you use wood be sure it is fairly dense otherwise it will not easily key.

> ***In this basic simulacra spell, we are going to use an apple.***

Using simulacra allows you to do magical procedures on people and things you are not in direct physical contact with. In fact the person or thing that you affect can be all the way on the other side of the world, or you can affect a global situation.

> ***Note: As with all spell work, record everything in your book of shadows. Also remember that magic is a precision science and altered procedures produce altered results!***

In this case, we'll use an apple as the main simulacra. Later, after you have used this spell several times, you can decide whether to stick with an apple or use some other kind of fruit... or some other kind of object altogether!

HOW DO YOU USE AN APPLE IN WITCHCRAFT AND MAGIC?

Now how do you use an apple as a magical tool?

Easy.

You simply "key" the apple to anything that you want to shrink, whether it is your level of body fat or a chronic bad habit that you can't seem to shake. In case you have not read the first two books in this Witchcraft Spell Books series, keying creates a correlation or psychic connection between an object—in this case an apple—and a situation, person, or thing. In other words, keying magically "programs" the apple.

In this basic spell, you will put the apple on a keyed Plate, and allow it to wither slowly over time. As the apple withers, the situation to which you've keyed the fruit will also shrink. An apple makes a good simulacrum in this case because it withers at a slow and believable rate. To be effective, the process of change in to simulacrum object has to progress at a believable rate.

Try to push simulacra magic too fast and it will backfire on you. For instance, an apple can take several weeks or months to fully wither, which is appropriate for shrinking certain problems (like body fat!). Using a bowl of melting ice cream, on the other hand, to represent the process of melting body fat would be much less effective since it would be difficult for your body to shed as fast as the ice cream would melt.

What You Will Need for the Magical Apple Ritual

- a fresh apple of your choice
- a Sun Candle
- paper or wooden matches
- a compass
- a Plate made of ceramic (salad or dinner size), preferably of Grass Green (bright spring green)
- pen and paper

Before you can set your spell into motion, you will need to obtain and key a Plate. Like other magical tools, such as objects used as simulacra, your Plate needs to be keyed for this spell to be effective. With magical tools, keying clears any impure energy from your Plate and aligns all the molecules so the energy flows in a particular direction and personalizes the Plate to you so that other people cannot easily use it.

The Plate, known in magical circles as a Shield or Pantacle, is the tool used to handle Earth energies. It is known as a Shield because it is often used magically to shield various operations against outside interference. Any small magical objects, such as talismans or pendulums, stored on a keyed Plate will be magically protected. In this case, we use a Plate to prevent interference with your spell and to keep the spell energies focused on the apple.

HOW TO QUICK-KEY YOUR PLATE

Because this is a guide on spell casting for beginners, we will use the "quick key" method for the Plate. The quick key method is easy, simple, and requires no other tools. The more complex Firebowl keying technique requires much more time and energy, and for this simple spell the quick key works equally well.

To quick key your Plate, place your hands on either side of the Plate, gripping the Plate with your thumbs on the top surface of the Plate and the rest of your fingers supporting the underside of the Plate. While looking at a Grass Green (bright spring green) color source, begin flowing Grass Green energy from your dominant hand through the Plate into your other hand.

Keep the energy flowing up your arm, across your shoulders, down the arm of your dominant hand (the hand with which you point). Flow the Earth energy out your output hand again. Circulate Grass Green for about three minutes, then pull your Earth energy back into your body. You will have a temporarily keyed Plate. Your Plate should feel slightly tingly, heavy, warm, or loaded. It will definitely feel different than before you keyed it.

Note that you will need to quick key your Plate every day until your spell is complete.

WRITING DIRECTORS AND LIMITERS FOR MAGICAL APPLES

Once you have keyed your Plate, you will need to decide whether you want to write a set of directors and limiters for this spell. We strongly recommend that you do take the time to write directors and limiters since magic *is* a precision science, and the more precise you are in your instructions to the Universe, the more likely you are to get your desired outcome. The only exception to this rule of thumb is if your situation is *so* simple that your Directors and Limiters would be two lines or less.

If you want to write directors and limiters, refer to the following section on "What are Directors and Limiters?" Take your time, think it through, and do it right. The Universe will do exactly as you ask it to do, so ask for precisely what you want—nothing more, nothing less. Once you have written your directors and limiters on a clean sheet of paper, fold it if necessary so it fits easily on the Plate, and place it on the Plate. Then proceed to the section that follows.

WHAT ARE DIRECTORS AND LIMITERS?

Now we just need to teach you how to write directors and limiters. Directors and limiters are no big deal. Directors are what you want your spell to do. Limiters are what you do *not* want your spell to do (such as cause harm or death to someone).

Specifically, directors and limiters specify the what, how, and when factors of a spell. You always need to specify directors and limiters for candle and Tarot spells (we will cover only a simple candle spell in this book).

Directors and limiters program your simple candle spell in terms of:

- the purpose of the spell
- how certain elements and energies are to be used
- the safeguards on the spell
- when the spell will start and stop

Specify anything that is important in your directors and limiters. For instance, if you are writing a spell for a new job you may want to specify the job description, amount of pay, type of company you want to be involved with, what kinds of benefits are involved, when you want the new job to start, the type of boss you want, and so forth.

Anything you don't specify is left to chance and spells usually follow the path of least resistance. Without directors and limiters you may achieve your goal but the spell may use methods that are illegal, dangerous, or harmful to self and others. The directors and limiters should almost be legalese. Think the way a lawyer might think when working on a contract. You don't have to put anything in your directors and limiters that you will do yourself, such as research on property values before buying a piece of property.

One student developed and launched a spell for a new job without specifying in her directors and limiters that her salary come from legal means. She ended up with an ideal job, wonderful working conditions, and co-workers she loved. She had to quit the job, though, when she discovered that she was working for the Mafia.

If your spell involves other people be sure that the directors and limiters are not binding (i.e. taking away a person's choice or forcing them to do something against their will). If you feel that someone's attitudes will affect your spell, you can set up a limiter preventing that person's attitude from affecting the spell or invite powers and beings to help.

Do not try to modify that person's behavior by binding them. Avoid enforcers, which are factors that force you to live your life a certain way, in your directors and limiters. For instance, a student once specified that the Universe not bring him more business than he could emotionally handle. After he launched the spell he broke up with his girlfriend and became an emotional wreck. The Universe therefore sent him absolutely no business!

When specifying numbers in your directors and limiters (such as age, salary, size, etc.), use a range rather than a single number so that your spell has more freedom to achieve the goal. Also, make sure your directors are reasonable. One student asked for $10,000 to manifest immediately. This is not reasonable. A spell is an energy matrix that gathers force and overcomes barriers over time—it rarely works right away. If you ask for something impossible you nullify the spell immediately.

An Esoteric School teacher once did a Tarot spell to prevent a bill from passing that would stop the sale of all supplements. It had already passed in the Senate and had a majority in the House. It was coming through to finalization in the House. The teacher did the spell and for two years nothing happened. Then, the day that the bill came before the House, the congressman who proposed the bill pulled it. The spell actualized in a single hour, two years after it was launched! The moral of this story is to be patient!

In the beginning, design your spells to create relatively small effects over a fairly short period of time. As you gain experience you can increase the content and reach of your spells.

Use limiters to program start and stop perimeters into the spell. You can even specify a delayed starting time for the spell using a limiter. You may also want to put in a standard limiter that says, "No one shall suffer harm, untimely death, or loss of property as the result of this spell," or something similar. It blocks the spell from taking certain harmful pathways in achieving its goal.

SAMPLE DIRECTORS AND LIMITERS

To give you an idea of how to write directors and limiters, here are some examples to get you started!

MONEY SPELL – DIRECTORS AND LIMITERS

1. To bring at least $10,000.00 in four to five weeks, by September 1st, xxxx, and not more than one million dollars by December xxxx, although the upper limit-date may later be extended.

2. No harm shall come to anyone, nor untimely death, nor loss of property as a result of this spell.

3. Whatever money shall come as a result of this spell shall be free and clear, with no strings attached.

4. The money will be used to pay off debts, to start my new career, and to purchase a house.

5. The spell will be open to support, help, and empowerment from angels and higher beings that can make a positive contribution.

6. My attitudes and fears will not have an adverse affect on this spell.

HOUSE LOCATING SPELL, DIRECTORS AND LIMITERS

1. To locate a house available for rent in or near XXXX, Colorado – available for rent between the start of this spell and up through first week of May, xxxx.
2. House will have at least four bedrooms and two bathrooms (full baths), plus a large kitchen with a side-by-side refrigerator or space for same.
3. House will have at least a two-car garage and a yard at least as large as xxxxx, and/or larger.
4. House will be available at least for two years, and the rent will not exceed $x,xxx a month with no penalty for late payment.
5. The landlord is to be local and honest, cooperative, friendly, and open-minded.
6. Our dog will be welcome and the area will be safe for her, not close to a busy street.
7. The space will work well for my healing business, with no legal restrictions or attitudes that oppose that.
8. The property will be of a sacred and spiritual nature for harmonious living for all of us.
9. The spell will help xxxx and xxxx in their search and work well with powers and beings (allies).

SPELL TO INCREASE HEALING AND MASSAGE PRACTICE, DIRECTORS AND LIMITERS

1. One shift at xxxx per week

2. Four to six hours at xxxx
3. Three to fourteen hours a week private practice
4. No more than five treatments a day – five days a week
5. Yearly income: $40,000-$60,000
6. Referrals from current clients
7. Clients of decency who respect and appreciate my work
8. Clients dependable and willing to pay
9. Changes to occur within three to four months of spell initiation.

HOW TO DO MAGICAL APPLES

Now that you have done all the preparatory steps of keying your Plate and writing directors and limiters, follow these steps to do the magical apple ritual:

1. Now you will need to key the apple to the problem or situation that you want to reduce. To key your apple, hold it in your dominant hand (the hand with which you point) while you think about everything you can about the situation.

   If you have difficulty focusing in this way, unfold and read aloud your list of directors and limiters in a voice of command. Otherwise, just use your intention.

For instance, if you want to reduce your debt, think about the name of the individual or company to whom you owe the debt, focus on the specific amount owed, recall the amount you pay each month... and so on. The more detailed you can get, the more accurately the apple will be keyed to your situation. In addition to thoughts, you can and should also flow emotions into the apple. Flow the feelings you have about the debt, be it fear, shame, guilt, anger, irritation, or hate.

2. When the apple feels charged, full, warm, heavy, tingly, or otherwise different in a magical or energetic sense, it is charged and ready for use. Put the apple on top of your keyed Plate and on top of your folded list of Directors and Limiters.

DAILY MAINTENANCE OF THIS SPELL

Since your Plate is quick keyed rather than permanently keyed, you will need to quick key it each day for your Plate to stay keyed. While this may seem like an inconvenience, in actuality the need to rekey your Plate daily gives you an opportunity to restate your intentions.

We suggest that after you do your daily rekeying of your Plate, you read your directors and limiters aloud while holding the apple in your dominant hand. This adds energy to the relationship between the situation and the apple, and strengthens your magical spell.

Finally, be patient. The goal of this spell is to achieve a permanent and lasting result. These kinds of magical results take time, energy, and daily maintenance. Expect this kind of spell to take weeks or even a few months. Negative energy like impatience will only hinder your spell, so be careful that you are in a positive mood when you do your daily rekeying and restating of Directors and Limiters!

HOW TO AVOID DOUBT

If you feel doubtful about whether your spell is working, ask the Universe for a sign that your spell is working. Then start looking for the different ways that the Universe is trying to speak to you.

One of the things we love most about magic is the many and varied ways it shows up in our lives. Many times when we ask for magical help from powers and beings, we are often surprised at the ways it shows up in our lives.

We also realize that many people miss the signs of magic in their lives because they don't know what to look for. In other words, magic is constantly sending messages to us, but we often overlook these signs and symbols.

To remind ourselves of these signs and symbols, as well as to help others who are looking for help from magic, we have compiled a list of the various ways magic has come into our lives over the years.

This is just a short excerpt, and we hope this helps to open your senses to the many ways magic is speaking to you.

SOME OF THE WAYS MAGIC SPEAKS TO US

- A sentence in a book that we open to a random page
- A check in the mail
- A conversation we overhear between two strangers
- A raven flying overhead, squawking a message
- The moral of a movie coinciding with a request for magical help
- A business phone call from a stranger, who turns out to be reading the same spiritual book as us
- Life-threatening surgery that forever changed perspectives on life
- Watching the amazing transformation in a child's behavior in 10 days
- A long-time friend leaving our lives, opening a new space for ...?
- A dream just before awakening
- Runes cast at just the right time, showing the way
- Meeting a group of magical practitioners meditating in the "cone of silence" at a mountain rest stop,
- Seeking and finding the Gurdjieff Work
- Taking one dose of a flower remedy made from the

magical datura plant

- Feeling the brush of angel wings while at a rest stop after an extremely long drive
- The reincarnation of our dog, Tether, who lived two lifetimes with us
- A nasty note from an anonymous person saying, "Learn how to park, idiot!"
- The planting and cultivation of the garden each year
- A call out of the blue from a long-lost friend
- Finding exactly what is wanted in a thrift store
- Getting what we want
- Not getting what we want
- Realizing that a negative influence in our lives was gone ... and that we hadn't even noticed its absence for months
- Rain arriving on a parched summer day
- A fender-bender that led to a successful business relationship
- Sitting with a wish for the longing to cease ... and having it cease
- Feeling the joy of not expressing dislike
- A misdirected email in our inbox, telling us just what we need to know
- Feeling lonely and realizing that we asked for sacred space
- Having a conversation in which no one understood a word that was said

- A magical ride on a huge white mule named H.B. (short for HoneyBun) through enchanting Zion National Park

Many of these magical messages have meaning only for us and probably don't make sense to you. That's the whole point of this list. Magic always speaks to us in very personal ways—ways that only make sense to us and have no meaning for anyone else.

As this list also demonstrates, magic sometimes speaks to us through contrast—through events that we would normally perceive as negative. Our job, as practitioners, is to question events that appear negative on the surface, and see whether the event answers some request we have made for magical help. One question to ask is, "What did I get from this event? What did I give up or give away?"

A Magical Challenge

We challenge you to make your own list of events through which magic speaks to you. You may have to dig a little to find these events. Trust us that the process will definitely be educational. Look through past events and see whether you can uncover magical messages or answers to prayer requests.

In the coming days, become more aware of your environment. If a raven passes overhead and squawks, look up the magical message that the raven carries in the book, *Medicine Cards: The Discovery of Power Through the Ways of Animals*, by Jamie Sams, David Carson, and Angela C. Werneke. If you are standing behind an exceptionally rude person at the grocery store checkout, see how the event might relate to the magic you are doing in your life. If nothing is happening in your life, ask yourself the magical meaning of such silence. Most of all, enjoy. That's what magic is for!

11.2

More Complex Rituals and Spells

Healing with the Magical Plate

In this section you will learn how to use a quick keyed magical Plate to heal yourself and others. The Plate is a magical tool with many healing properties, being the tool of Mother Earth and Earth energies. All you will need for the rituals outlined in this section are your Plate and the person you seek to heal (yourself or another person).

You can use your quick keyed Plate to deliver concentrated blasts of Grass Green and Earth Brown energies for healing. You will need to quick key your Plate each time you want to use it for healing.

The Plate can handle and output more energy than we can transmit directly with our hands, which makes it a wonderful magical tool for healing.

HOW THE MAGICAL PLATE WORKS

To effectively use your Plate for healing you need to understand how the Plate projects energy. When you push energy into your Plate, it gathers from the edges inward, forming a cone that tapers down to a thin beam. The cone projected by most Plates is around 18 inches long (see the following figure).

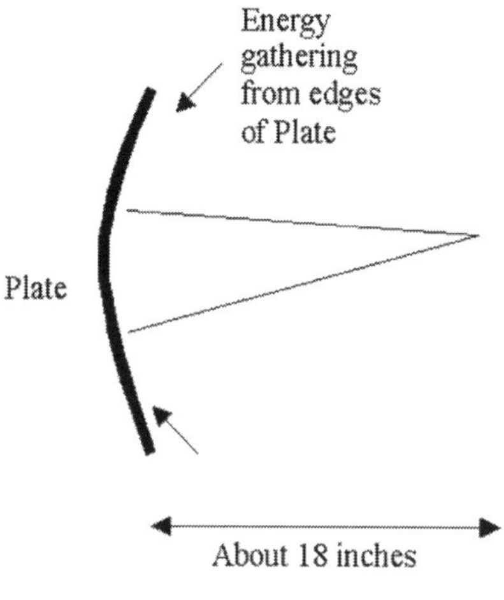

HOW TO HEAL WITH THE PLATE

It's a good idea to practice projecting beams of Grass Green from your Plate on yourself. Do not use Earth Brown until you have more experience, since this color can produce permanent unanticipated effects.

HOW TO PRACTICE USING YOUR PLATE

1. Hold your plate by placing your hands on either side of the Plate, gripping the Plate with your thumbs on the top surface of the Plate and the rest of your fingers supporting the underside of the Plate. Position your Plate so that the back of the Plate faces toward the ceiling, and the front (the surface on which food is normally placed) is pointed at your thigh.

3. Pull Grass Green energy in through your elbows or shoulder blades.

4. Push it down your arms and into the Plate through your thumbs.

5. As you flow Grass Green energy through your Plate, move your Plate back and forth over your thigh. Keep moving your Plate until you get a precise feel for the length and shape of the beam that your Plate projects. With Grass Green energy you will feel itching and weaving as the beam hits your body. Once you've practiced on yourself you can use your

Plate for the types of healing outlined in the following sections.

HEALING BRUISES

For a bad bruise that's starting to heal, you can use your Plate to flow Grass Green into the area to promote healing and cellular regeneration.

SMOTHERING TUMORS

You can smother tumors with beams of Earth Brown from your Plate. The benefit of using your Plate is that it won't produce as much inflammation as an Athame (the magical knife). The Earth Brown energy will solidify the tumor into a hard lump, which you can then break up and wash away with your Chalice. NEVER use Grass Green on tumors. Tumors are already too healthy and Grass Green will only accelerate the growth process.

STOPPING INTERNAL BLEEDING

With forms of internal bleeding, such as ulcers, using your Plate is an excellent solution. Use your Plate to put some Earth Brown energy into the area. Once the area stops bleeding the person may have a lump in their stomach. Flow some Grass Green into the area to start the healing process and allow the natural Air and Water energies in the stomach to soften and dissolve the lump. For ulcers the Earth Brown energy will help to block out the acids that are dissolving the stomach lining. Do not use Earth Brown energy in the heart, lung or throat areas. It is too heavy for these organs and will smother them.

STOPPING EXTERNAL BLEEDING

Use Earth Brown energies from your Plate to slow the flow of blood from external wounds. Flow Earth Brown into the area until the bleeding stops. Do not add Grass Green energy since Grass Green tends to accelerate flow, which would increase the flow of blood. Wait a few days until the wound is completely closed over and stable, then add in a little Grass Green energy to start the healing process. If the wound starts bleeding again you've added the Grass Green too soon. Add more Earth Brown energies to stabilize the area then wait a few more days before adding Grass Green.

HEALING BROKEN BONES

You can heal broken bones, once they are properly set, with your Plate. Begin by flowing Grass Green energy into the break to start the healing process. The person will experience the knitting or weaving sensation that always accompanies bone growth. Afterward, flow some Earth Brown energies into the area to stabilize it. If the person goes to the hospital to have the bone set be sure they don't get a hard cast. Hard casts tend to slow the healing process and you can't work on the break with your Plate through a hard cast. A removable cast is much more conducive to healing since you may need to add Grass Green into the break daily.

11.3

More Complex Rituals and Spells

Pendulum Clearings

Has a life-problem suddenly cropped up? Do you need a quickie solution to fix the problem before it becomes a catastrophe? Then try the easy pendulum clearing ritual. With this ritual, you can literally take the pendulum of your choice, swing it in circles for a while, and consider your problem solved. In fact, you don't just have to consider the problem solved, you can watch it be solved right before your eyes.

For instance, one of our students was running late for a very important meeting with her boss. Her boss hated when people were late, and heavily penalized people who showed up late. More importantly, the meeting was about her annual performance review.

Showing up late was simply not an option! And yet, our student found herself stuck in traffic with a dead cell phone. She was about to panic.

But instead, she kept her cool and, instead of panicking, she whipped out her pendulum. Sitting amongst a gaggle of non-moving cars, she spun her pendulum on the sly (so other drivers wouldn't think she was crazy!). She asked that the pendulum "unwind" the problem. As soon as the pendulum stopped spinning, she considered her problem solved.

When she arrived at her meeting, her boss' secretary informed her that her boss had gotten a sudden case of food poisoning, and had gone home. The secretary had left a message on the student's dead cell phone, but of course the student could not listen to the message. The point was, however, that the boss never knew that our student was late to her meeting, and the secretary volunteered to keep the secret.

Problem solved! That was easy, right? You can use this same ritual anytime life throws you a monkey-wrench and you need a solution... fast.

All you need for this ritual is a pendulum. We will describe the parameters of a pendulum, as well as how to make and train your own pendulum so that you get accurate answers and help. Finally, we will give you specific instructions on how "spin away your troubles" using your pendulum!

WHAT IS A PENDULUM?

A pendulum is any lightweight object suspended from a string or chain. It is a magical tool that becomes a natural extension of you, and can access any and all information that exists in the Universe. You just have to know which questions to ask.

For instance, a pendulum can reveal your body's own native wisdom. It can indicate whether certain supplements or flower essences will improve your health. It can also reveal whether a health problem stems from a particular organ or an emotional source. Dowsing with a pendulum is a simple form of magic that has a remarkable number of applications.

HOW TO MAKE YOUR OWN PENDULUM

You can easily buy a pendulum, but many practitioners prefer to make their own pendulums. Anyone can make a pendulum. You just need a lightweight object plus a chain or some string.

You can use paper clips, small rocks, earrings, hairpins,

pendants, small medallions, crystals, and talismans. If you want to use a crystal, use an amethyst, and store any kind of crystal you use in a pewter box, which protects it from negative energy. Don't use Aurora crystals, which have been treated with petroleum (and thus work poorly as pendulums).

If you choose to hang your pendulum on a chain, use a silver chain, which is the most magically stable metal. You can also hang your pendulum on any kind of natural fiber such as cotton or silk, horse or human hair, or leather.

TRAINING YOUR PENDULUM FOR DOWSING AND OTHER MAGICAL PROCEDURES

Once you have made your pendulum your next step is to train it so that it answers your questions quickly and accurately. Follow these steps to train your pendulum.

1. First cleanse your pendulum with smoke from a charged cedar/sage smudge stick. To charge your smudge stick, sit in the South and face North. Light the stick with paper or wooden matches. When the stick is producing a thick, dense column of smoke, say aloud in a voice of command:

Fire and Air where you are cast,

Let no spell nor adverse purpose last,

Not in accord with me!

Cleanse this tool and cleanse its space,

Far from here send baneful trace!

Hold your pendulum in the column of smoke, keeping it there until the smoke sticks to all parts of the pendulum. Once the smoke sticks, the pendulum has been magically cleansed. A used pendulum, or a pendulum made from objects with "junky" energy, may take up to five minutes to be cleansed. Be patient. The smoke will eventually stick.

2. Next, key your pendulum so that it responds to your energies. To key it, hold your pendulum in your dominant hand (the hand with which you point). Flow energy into the pendulum for a minute or two, or until it grows warm and tingly.

3. Begin training your pendulum by establishing its "yes" and "no" directions. Decide if you want your pendulum to indicate "yes" with a vertical or horizontal swing. The "no" indicator will be the opposite of the "yes" indicator (if "yes" is a vertical swing, then "no" is a horizontal swing).

   It's often easier to use your pendulum while sitting, so get in a comfortable position and hold your pendulum suspended from your dominant hand. Make sure the pendulum is on a long enough chain or string to swing freely. Rest your elbow on a table or your knee to stabilize your hand.

Swing your pendulum in a gentle clockwise circle and tell it, "Show me yes." Wait for the pendulum to settle into the proper swing (whatever direction you chose). If it doesn't, ask again.

Once your pendulum consistently swings in the proper direction for "yes," use the same process to ask it to show you the proper swing for "no."

4. Finally, start training your pendulum to give you actual answers by practicing asking questions about short futures. Ask yes/no questions that can be verified in a 15 to 30 minute time frame. For instance, at the end of the work day you might ask your pendulum, "Will my roommate be home in the next 20 minutes?" Verify the correctness of your pendulum's answer, and then ask another question.

It actually does not matter whether your pendulum gives you the correct answer or not at first. It is more important to give your pendulum a lot of practice with questions about short futures. The more your work with your pendulum, the more accurate it will become. Don't get obsessed with your early results

How to Do Pendulum Clearings

One of the best things you can do with a pendulum is clear problems or snags in your life. Do the following steps to perform pendulum clearings.

1. Hold your pendulum in your dominant hand, letting it dangle while you visualize the problem you want to clear.

2. Ask your pendulum, "Can I, may I, should I, clear this situation?" If you get a yes answer from your pendulum, then move forward. You can use an indicator plate later to ask your pendulum more complex questions (see the indicator plate provided following this section).

3. Begin swinging your pendulum in a counter clockwise direction (the direction of unwinding), asking it to clear the situation. As you do this, "see" the situation resolving in your mind. Be very specific with your request and what you envision as to the situation being resolved.

4. Continue to focus on clearing the situation until your pendulum stops spinning in the counter clockwise direction. It will then either start moving along a vertical or horizontal axis, stop or start spinning clockwise. When it stops swinging counter clockwise on its own then the problem has been cleared.

Once a problem has been cleared, you might unconsciously bring it back by fretting about it. Trust the power of your pendulum and your intent, and release the problem from your consciousness. If you find it seeping back into your consciousness throughout the day, change your focus to something else.

You can use this same pendulum exercise to clear repetitive thoughts that you find yourself having. Instead of visualizing a situation you want resolved just hold the repetitive thought in your mind. Ask your pendulum to clear the thought from your life. After the process, you may still find the thought popping up in your mind occasionally, but it should appear far less frequently than before, and eventually will disappear... just like magic!

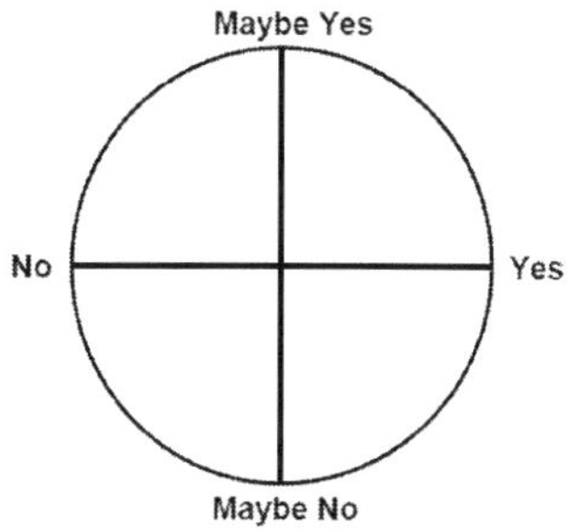

PENDULUM INDICATOR PLATE

ASKING THE RIGHT QUESTIONS

At this stage, your pendulum can answer any yes/no question. To increase the accuracy of your pendulum's answers, check the way you question your pendulum. How you phrase your questions will determine the accuracy of the answers. The general principle for asking questions in pendulum magic, as in spell work, is, "Be precise!"

For instance, if you ask your pendulum, "Will it rain today?" and your pendulum says, "Yes," don't be surprised if you don't see a drop of rain that day. Was your pendulum wrong? No. It probably rained somewhere in the world that day. Since you didn't ask for a precise location, your pendulum could not give you a precise answer.

As with everything else, practice makes perfect when it comes to pendulum magic. To remind yourself to practice, take your pendulum with you in your pocket or purse (wrapped in a piece of silk or in a small pouch) and use it any time you have a few minutes to yourself. You'll be surprised at how many opportunities you will have to use it!

11.4

More Complex Rituals and Spells

Sending Messages with the Magical Chalice

Have you ever had something you really need to talk to someone about, but you are not sure how to go about it. It could be something you are dissatisfied about at work and don't think your boss will be receptive to discussing. Or maybe you need to tell a friend something, but you know they may become defensive. Or it could be you have had a disagreement or argument with someone, and are not sure how to approach them to straighten things out.

Don't worry. You can still communicate with these people without ever having to say a single thing to them directly. There are many magical tools with which you communicate with others on a Spirit-to-Spirit level.

Messages can be sent to people with the Wand, which is the Air tool. However, if you want a deeper level communication—or you want to access someone on their emotional level—using the Chalice is the best choice. The Chalice is the Water element magical tool, and Water is the element associated with emotions.

WHAT YOU WILL NEED TO SEND MESSAGES WITH THE MAGICAL CHALICE

- a Sun Candle
- paper or wooden matches
- a Chalice (description to follow)

HOW TO CHOOSE A MAGICAL CHALICE

For this ritual you will need a Chalice, the magical tool of the Water element. These tips should help you choose an appropriate Chalice. Your Chalice should:

- be a goblet-shaped drinking cup that has a stem for easy handling.
- have a good-sized bowl (you will want to be able to store small objects in your Chalice for magical protection). The bowl can have patterns on it as long as the patterns are not too deep.
- be made of only one material. Avoid combinations of material, such as glass and metal. Glass and ceramic work best, although you can also use Chalices made of silver, pewter, or copper. Some people prefer clear glass because you can see what is in the Chalice, and other people prefer Water Blue (bright blue) Chalices since we often use Water Blue in working with the Chalice. Wood Chalices do not work well because they have too much Air element in them.

KEYING YOUR CHALICE

The first thing to do with your Chalice, just as with any magical tool, is to key it. Keying it clears any impure energy and aligns the molecules so that the energy flows in a particular direction. It also personalizes the tool to you.

Before you can use your Chalice to send messages to another person on an emotional or spiritual level, you need to key it. Follow these steps to "quick key" your Chalice:

1. Cup your hands on either side of the bowl part of the Chalice.
2. Locate a Water Blue (bright blue) color source.
3. Looking at the Water Blue color source for reference, begin circling Water Blue from your output (dominant) hand through the Chalice to your input (non-dominant) hand. Continue moving the energy up your input arm, across your shoulders, down your output arm, and out your output hand again.
4. Circulate the color Water Blue for approximately three minutes, and then pull your Water energy back into your body.
5. This will create a temporarily keyed Chalice.

HOW TO SEND MESSAGES WITH THE MAGICAL CHALICE

Chalice messages affect the emotions and can be very strong as they literally shoot out of your Chalice like water from a fire hose. They can become quite compulsive so you should make sure you are following Rules of the Road when sending these types of messages. The Rules of the Road say not to bind anyone. If you send a compulsive message then you are breaking this rule.

For example, if you send a strong message of "Stay home!" to someone, the person may not be able to leave their house for days. Think through your messages, as in any magical procedure, and keep these types of message short and simple. There are other techniques to send longer messages or hold entire psychic conversations with people, such as the Water Bowl technique discussed in Book II of this series. Note that in this ritual, you will use ***Water energy*** rather than ***actual water*** from your Chalice to send messages. Follow these steps to send messages with your Chalice:

1. Sit in the South facing North with your materials before you.

2. Light and charge your Sun Candle, waiting for the candle to achieve a working flame before proceeding to the next step.

3. Move to the East with your Sun Candle and Chalice. Sit facing East. Hold your keyed Chalice in your output (dominant) hand with thumb and forefinger around the bowl part, and the rest of your fingers wrapped around the stem.

4. Extend your output arm straight out to your side at shoulder height, keeping the top (open end) of the Chalice pointing at the ceiling.

5. Now bend your output arm so that it forms a 90 degree angle at the elbow. With your output arm in this position, keep the top of the Chalice pointing toward the ceiling.

6. Pull Water Blue energy (from a Water Blue color source) into your elbow of your output arm, and push that energy into the Chalice.
7. Look in the direction of your output arm, and visualize the face of the person to whom you are sending the message. Visualize the person's face about five feet away from you, at your shoulder height.
8. Straighten your output arm at the elbow with your palm up. Keep your output arm, now straightened, level with your shoulder. In this position, the Chalice will now be resting on its side in your up-facing palm. The top (open end) of the Chalice will now be pointed at your visualized image of the message recipient's face. Allow the Water energy that you have stored in your arm flow into the Chalice.
9. Shoot a beam of Water Blue at the visualization of the person's face while saying your message out loud. It is very important to do this with your palm facing up, since Chalice messages are already very compelling. A message sent with the palm down could become an enforcer—meaning the message could actually force the recipient to take action against his or her will.
10. Blow out your Sun Candle. Store both your Chalice and Sun Candle.

Chalice messages can be a very effective way to start communication with someone that you feel uneasy about approaching. The message may need to be repeated multiple times before you see a noticeable effect as there are many blocks that can be encountered in the other person. Just remember to think it through, keep it simple, and have fun with the process.

11.5

MORE COMPLEX RITUALS AND SPELLS

GETTING RID OF THE UNWANTED WITH THE FIREBOWL BURN

One of the best Fire magic spells around is the Firebowl Burn. A Firebowl is exactly what it sounds like—a bowl that contains Fire, or magical Fire energy. Specifically, a Firebowl is an essential magical tool that can be used for cleansing, divination, message-sending, full-cast circles, and many other types of beginner and advanced magical spells.

In this section we will teach you how to use a Firebowl to get rid of anything unwanted in your life. The Firebowl Burn is a simple spell that is also very effective.

While the use of the Firebowl does require more materials than most of the spells taught in this book, you will find that having the Firebowl in your magical toolkit is a very handy thing indeed!

WHAT YOU WILL NEED FOR THE FIREBOWL BURN

- **Firebowl**: see the description in the following section
- **Ground fire clay** or clean, fine sand. Non-scented cat litter, which is ground fire clay, works well for this as long as it does not have chemicals or deodorants in it. You will need enough to put one to two inches in the bottom of your Firebowl as an insulator to protect the Firebowl itself, your hands, and any surfaces from the heat.
- **Self-starting charcoal**, which can be purchased from religious supply stores or online. The round charcoals with bowl-shaped depressions in the middle are best.
- **Wooden or paper matches**. Use only wooden or paper matches to light your candles and charcoals.

The scent and energetic side-bands associated with butane and other petroleum products change the Fire energies you are working with.

- **Finely chopped or shaved wood chips** or tree bark. These are used to insulate the charcoal from the tree resin or incense, and to facilitate the burning of the materials in your Firebowl.
- **Pine resin**. You can collect pine resin yourself, or purchase it.
- **Finely ground or rubbed sage**. If you collect sage, you can grind it in a blender or coffee grinder. You can also purchase it in many online stores or health food stores.
- **Sun Candle**
- **Pen and plenty of blank paper**

HOW TO CHOOSE YOUR FIREBOWL

The best Firebowls for magical uses have these characteristics:

- made of brass, cast-iron, ceramic or a hard hardwood
- four to six inches in diameter (or larger, since the

Firebowl Burn requires the Firebowl to be able to contain burning paper)

- four to five inches deep
- a shape that is easily held with one or both hands
- light enough to carry in one hand if necessary
- stable when placed on a flat surface
- slightly curved-in and flared back out at the top rim to promote "columning" of incense or smoke (see the following figure)

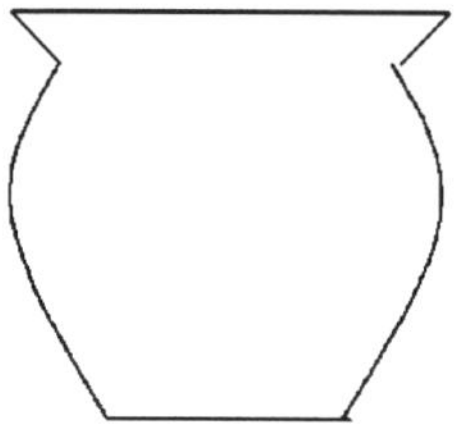

IDEAL FIREBOWL PROFILE

HOW TO PREPARE AND CHARGE THE FIREBOWL

Charging the Firebowl programs it for a specific purpose, such as cleansing a space, person, or object. Since magic is a precision science, charging your Firebowl for certain operations can make this a much more effective magical tool. Charging states the intended purpose and programs that purpose into the tool. Charging is not an invocation or prayer to spirit-beings or deities, just a program.

You don't have to key a Firebowl before you use it (keying aligns the energies in a tool and personalizes it for your use). The Firebowl keys itself every time you light it.

Before charging your Firebowl, prepare it with the proper materials. Read through these materials and prepare your Firebowl. Print out the instructions for charging the Firebowl, and then proceed with the Firebowl Burn!

PREPARE THE FIREBOWL

1. Fill the bottom of the Firebowl with one to two inches of sand or clay.

2. Place a block of unlit self-starting charcoal in the center of the bed of sand or clay.

3. Have your wood shavings, sage, and resin ready to put onto the charcoal after it is lit. Make sure your pine resin is broken into small pieces that can easily be added onto the wood shavings.

4. Light your Sun Candle with wooden or paper matches, and then charge the candle using the following charge verse:

Getting Rid of the Unwanted with the Firebowl Burn

Child of Wonder,

Child of Flame,

Nourish My Spirit,

And Protect My Aim!

Charge the Firebowl

1. Stand or sit in the South facing North with your Firebowl and other materials in front of you.

2. Light the charcoal from the flame of the charged Sun Candle. It will begin sparking within seconds. If the charcoal is old or damp, you may need to use tongs to hold it over the candle flame for several minutes. Also, with old or damp charcoal, you may want to light the top of it in the center of the bowl-shaped depression so that the materials you put on top will burn more easily.

3. Once the charcoal is lit, place it back into the center of your Firebowl. Blow Sun Yellow energy, pulled from the Sun Candle, into the Firebowl.

4. Add wood shavings to the charcoal, then pine resin, then sage as needed until the Firebowl is producing a good column of smoke.

5. In a voice of command charge the Firebowl with the appropriate verse below, blowing Sun Yellow into the charcoal before and after the verse, and between each line of the verse.

Fire and Air where you are cast,

Let no spell nor adverse purpose last,

Not in accord with me!

Clear from my life these unwanted matters,

Send far from my life these negative factors!

Thus my will, so it be!

HOW TO DO THE FIREBOWL BURN

This is a wonderful ritual because it matches the energy of anger so well: it burns! Plus, it is really simple to do, not to mention highly satisfying. Just be sure to observe fire safety precautions before doing this magical ritual. Use this ritual whenever you feel angry or negative, or want to remove negative factors from your life. Follow these instructions to do the Firebowl Burn:

1. Seat yourself in the South facing North. Have all of your materials in front of you (including instructions on Charging the Firebowl).
2. Light and charge the Sun Candle.
3. Charge the Firebowl as per the instructions.

4. Now write everything that is bothering you or making you feel negative. Pour it all out on paper, as fast and furious as you can. Write as many pages as necessary, and feel free to repeat yourself as many times as you want. There's no limit. Write until you literally run out of steam (which is a combination of Fire and Water energy).

5. Now for the good part of this magic ritual—the big burn! Place your Firebowl in front of you (be sure your Firebowl is large enough to accommodate the burning of the papers—if not, move the entire operation to the sink or some other place that is safe for burning!).

Before you set your papers alight with your matches, take a moment to do whatever you need to move the anger out of you. Ask for help from angels, ask for guidance, or just have a moment of silence. Then, light up the papers and watch your anger go up in smoke. You can light each sheet individually (many people find this method more satisfying), or wad up the whole mess of papers and light the entire thing (again observing fire safety precautions).

Whatever you do with this magic ritual, enjoy the heck out of it. Be safe about your burning, and then enjoy, enjoy, enjoy! It's not often that we have permission to do somewhat destructive acts like this, so go ahead and milk it for all it's worth!

Note that if you are dealing with a chronic or stubborn problem, you may need to do the Firebowl Burn on a daily basis for 40 days or more. This will give you 40 days of making daily conscious contact with the Universe. This will also build the strength of your spell matrix for 40 days in a row. While some experts feel that bad habits or chronic conditions can be handled in less than 40 days, spiritually the number 40 is very effective.

If you choose to perform this ritual for 40 days, it is very important that you be committed to doing so! If you should miss a day, start over again. Don't worry... this will only add strength to your spell. The continuity of 40 days *in a row* will increase the power of this spell exponentially. This is true of any magical spell, ritual, or meditation. Plus, this continuous daily contact and exercise of intention will cause you to build up a vast reservoir of energy with which you can begin to manifest anything you desire.

11.6

More Complex Rituals and Spells

Touch Assist for Healing

Most of us know about the power of the healing touch. However, if you are not one of those people who was born just knowing how to "lay hands" on people and heal them, then the touch assist spell ritual can be of real help to you. The touch assist is a simple way that you can methodically heal an area of chronic pain or acute injury. The beauty of this spell ritual is that *anyone* can use it effectively, given that the instructions are followed exactly. You do not need anything but your hand (or possibly the rubber eraser end of a pencil) for this ritual.

TWO THINGS TO REMEMBER WHEN DOING TOUCH ASSIST

There are two things to keep in mind when using this technique:

1. Body energy flows are head-to-extremities, inside to outside, *and* back-to-front.

2. *Any* injury or energy problem in one side of the body produces a "resonance reflection" or mirroring in the other side (because all meridians are bi-lateral).

HOW TO DO THE TOUCH ASSIST

Follow these steps to do the Touch Assist:

1. Locate the problem area, and explain briefly about the Touch Assist to the person on whom you are working.

2. Have the person close their eyes.

3. Lightly touch the person five or six times at irregular intervals and random spots near to, but above or on the "head side" of the area in question (be sure to include the "resonance reflection" area). Each time you touch the person, say "Feel my finger," and acknowledge their response with "Okay," "Good," "All right," or "Thank you." In turn, the person should also respond each time with "Yes."

4. Next, move to spots that are on the "away from the head" side of the area, but still near the problem area. Do five or six touches there using the same communication sequence as above for each touch.

5. Finally, work *in* the area in question, including the "resonance reflection" area, using five to ten touches and the same communication sequence for each touch. Keep the communication fresh and lively—don't get mechanical! You want to keep the person's awareness or interest lively because this procedure brings awareness to places in the body that have no awareness. Mechanical words do not make completed communication cycles.

6. Once you're done, say "OK, that's it," and then ask the person to open their eyes. Have them check for sensations and function in the problem area.

ADDITIONAL NOTES ON TOUCH ASSIST

- If the area in question is relatively large, the number of touches should be increased to cover it.
- If the area in question is inside the trunk or torso of the body, working the mid-thighs (front, sides, and back of both thighs) will often be effective. The meridians that relate to the internal abdomen are on the thighs and lower legs.
- If the person checks and reports some abnormal sensations or lack of function still present in the problem area, do the procedure again.
- **To Administer Touch Assist to Self**: Substitute the blunt end of a pencil (or some similar object such as a capped pen or a piece of dowel) for your fingertip in making the touches.
- **As a Variant of Step 5** (particularly when dealing with "dead-spots"): After a number of touches (five to ten) in the area, begin by touching just the "nearest to head" side of the area (with the same communication sequence), tell the person to ***follow your finger***, and then "draw" it lightly *through* the area while repeatedly asking the person, "Can you still feel my finger?" Always acknowledge any communication from the person as before. If you get a "No," go back to where you last got a "Yes" and repeat the process. Go through the area five or six times in this manner. Then repeat the entire procedure in the "resonance reflection" area.

SOME ADDITIONAL THOUGHTS ON HEALING

Magical healing is one area of magic and witchcraft practice that can be truly tricky. Suppose you perform a magical healing ritual on someone or do a remote healing. The person gets better and you feel great.

But then the doubt creeps in. You begin wondering whether you were responsible for the healing or if the person was going to get better anyway. Or maybe your healing and the person's recovery were just coincidental—they just happened to occur at the same time. Or perhaps the person's angels and guides stepped in and performed the healing, and your magic had nothing to do with the person's recovery.

That kind of self-doubt most assuredly will drive you crazy and interfere with your ability to effectively practice magic. When it comes to practicing any kind of magic, here's one rule that will help you keep self-doubt out of the picture:

NEVER ALLOW YOUR MAGIC TO BE TESTED.

People who don't believe in magic will commonly challenge magic practitioners to "prove" their magic by passing certain tests. This does nothing but introduce self-doubt into your practice. This rule applies to you as well. Don't try to "test" your own magical abilities or try to figure out if you really healed someone.

The best position to take when it comes to magical healing is to realize that you are doing magic for your benefit and for the benefit of others, should they choose to make use of it. According to master dowser and healer, Harold McCoy, who has assisted in many miraculous healings, we are not and cannot be the sole instruments of remote healing. Healing is usually a combined effort between healer, client, and higher beings. If any part of this equation is missing, such as when the client refuses healing energy, healing will not occur. At the same time, when healing does occur, no single party in the equation is responsible. Instead, it's a group effort.

As Harold himself puts it:

> ***"I just do these things and the person gets better. I don't know that there is any connection, or what that may be, but it doesn't matter!"***

This is a failsafe position for magical healing. You know there is a connection between your magical act and the healing, but you don't have to know the exact nature of the connection. This lets you off the hook when it comes to self-doubt.

These are Harold's seven principles for magical healing work, which may help keep you from self-doubt when healing yourself or others:

1. Never turn anyone down.
2. Be always 100% committed.
3. Always get permission.

4. Always invoke your guides and angels.
5. Don't charge, but accept donations.
6. There are no failures.
7. We don't diagnose nor cure.

11.7

More Complex Rituals and Spells

Nighttime Blessing Ritual

This spell is appropriate since the night is the end of the day, and this spell marks the end of the guided directions in this book!

If you want to bring magic into your home and hearth, one of the best magic rituals for creating harmony within the family is the nighttime blessing ritual. This ritual is done at night, right before bed, with the whole family.

WHAT YOU WILL NEED FOR THE NIGHTTIME BLESSING RITUAL

- a Sun Candle
- paper or wooden matches
- a Chalice (see description from the earlier section of this book)
- sea salt
- spring water

HOW TO DO THE NIGHTTIME BLESSING RITUAL

This ritual is a peaceful, meditative ritual that helps to promote harmony and health in families and couples. Doing this ritual consistently each evening before bed can lead to calm, restful periods of sleep. If you don't have a partner to do this ritual with, you can do it with yourself or even your pets! Follow these steps to do this ritual:

1. Gather and place your materials in front of you. Sit in the South, facing North.

2. Charge your Sun Candle as instructed previously.

3. Fill the Chalice halfway with spring water, and sprinkle in a little salt.

4. Blow Water Blue (bright blue) energy into the Chalice as you swirl the water clockwise.

5. Say the verse below, blowing Water Blue into the Chalice as you swirl the water clockwise before and after the verse, and between each line of the verse:

   Water and Earth where you are cast,

   Let no spell nor adverse purpose last,

   Not in accord with me!

   Bless these people and bless their space,

   Far from here send baneful trace.

   Thus my will, so it be!

6. If you are doing this ritual alone, change the fourth line to "Bless this person and bless my space."

7. Hold the Chalice in your left hand, and face the person you are blessing (unless you are blessing yourself).

8. Dip the index finger of your right hand into the water, and draw a vertical line down the center of the person's forehead (or your own forehead). The line should be one to one-and-a-half inches long.

9. Draw a horizontal line of the same length from left to right through the center of the first line, forming a cross.

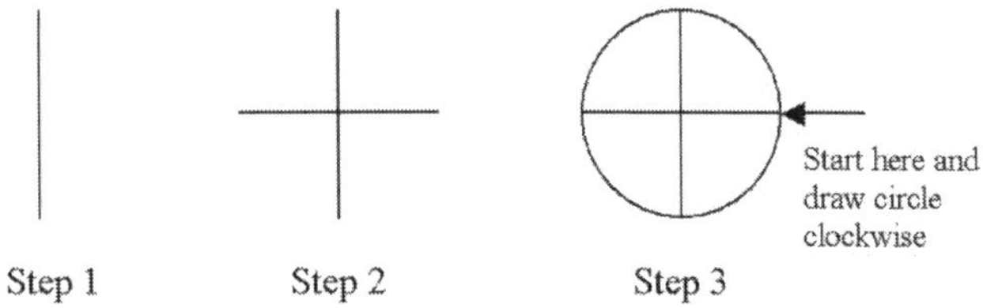

10. Starting at the right end of the horizontal line, draw a clockwise circle, touching both ends of both lines. As you draw the circle, say to the person, "For the peace of your mind." If you're doing the ritual alone say "For the peace of my mind."

11. Repeat the same procedure on the person's chest (or your own chest), over the heart. As you draw the circle, say, "For the joy of your heart." Substitute the words "my heart" if you are doing the ritual alone.

12. Ask the person to take a sip of water from the Chalice. As they sip, say, "And for the health of your body." If you're doing the ritual alone, take a sip and then say "And for the health of my body."

13. If there are two people participating in the ritual, reverse roles and repeat the process. If there are many people, one person can bless everyone, and then one person in the group blesses the first person.

14. You can use the alternate verses, "For the health of your mind," and "For the health of your Spirit."

Enjoy the restful peace that comes from this very ancient blessing ritual. You can also use this ritual anytime you are unhappy or unable to sleep.

12

Resources for the Practice of Witchcraft and Magic

Magical Resources and Online Store on the Esoteric School Website

http://www.shamanschool.com

Facebook

https://www.facebook.com/EsotericSchool

YouTube Channel

http://www.youtube.com/user/shamanschool

OTHER BOOKS IN THE "WITCHCRAFT SPELL BOOKS" SERIES

- Book One: Learn How to Do Witchcraft Rituals and Spells with Your Bare Hands
- Book Two: Learn How to Do Witchcraft Rituals and Spells with Household Ingredients
- Book Three: Learn How to Do Witchcraft Rituals and Spells with Magical Tools

About G. Alan Joel

Shamanic Healer and Doctor of Chinese Medicine

As co-founder of the Esoteric School of Shamanism and Magic, Mr. Joel has been a practitioner of witchcraft, magic, and shamanism for over three decades. A Doctor of Chinese Medicine and a shamanic healer, he uses remote healing to assist clients all over the world to recover on many levels (physical, mental, emotional, and spiritual). He employs a variety of witchcraft, shamanic, magical, and traditional Chinese Medicine practices—including many of the rituals and techniques described in this book.

Whether a practice is called witchcraft, magic, wicca, paganism, or shamanism, at the Esoteric School of Shamanism and Magic students and teachers study, research, and teach useful knowledge in these areas. As co-founder, Mr. Joel's goal is to empower as many people as possible from all over the globe to learn skills in witchcraft, magic, and shamanism.

7085353R00183

Printed in Great Britain
by Amazon.co.uk, Ltd.,
Marston Gate.